About the Author

Katharina Reiss was born on Ap
many where she concluded her h   _. uipioma
in 1940. From 1941 to 1944 she studied at the Interpreters' Institute
at the University of Heidelberg, receiving there her first degree as a
professional translator. She taught at the Heidelberg Interpreters'
Institute, Spanish Department, from 1944 to 1970. From 1951 to
1954, Katharina Reiss studied philology, receiving her doctorate in
that field in 1954. During the following years (1965-1970) she
headed up the Spanish Department of the Institute. In 1971, she
accepted an invitation from the University of Wuerzberg, where she
served as the Director of Academic Studies at the Seminar for Romance Languages. Her habilitation and degree followed in 1974, in
the field of Applied Linguistics, at the University of Mainz.

From 1974 onwards Katharina Reiss lectured on translation studies at the Germersheim campus of the University of Mainz. But she
had been speaking at conferences and at various universities in Germany and elsewhere since 1967. She served as translation consultant
to the United Bible Societies during the period 1980-1987. Although
officially retired in 1988, Reiss continues to lecture in Mainz. Her
publications include over 90 essays and reviews, with many translated into English, French, Spanish, Portuguese, Russian, Finnish,
Turkish and Chinese. Her books include *Möglichkeiten und
Grenzen der Übersetzungskritik* (1971, 1984), *Texttyp und Übersetzungsmethode* (1976, 1993), *Grundlegung einer allgemeinen
Übersetzungstheorie* (with Hans Vermeer, 1984, 1991) and
Grundfragen der Übersetzungswissenschaft (edited by M. Snell-
Hornby and M. Kadric, 1995).

Reiss also translated numerous books and articles from Spanish,
including works by Leopoldo Alas (Clarin), Vincente Blanco-
Ibariez, Pio Baroja, Jaime Ferrero Alemparte, Gustavo Beyhaut
and José Ortega y Gasset's classic "Miseria y Esplendor de la
traducción".

About the Translator

Dr. Erroll F. Rhodes, Associate Director/Scholarly Editorial in the Content Development Department of the American Bible Society, taught Japanese in the Army Specialized Training Program at the University of Chicago during the Second World War while working on his doctorate at the Divinity School. After the War he served for fourteen years as Professor of New Testament at St. Paul's (Rikkyo) University, Tokyo, also co-editing a Japanese translation of F. L. Cross, *The Early Christian Fathers* (1969). Since joining the staff of the American Bible Society in 1968 he has continued to contribute articles to periodicals and reference works on the history of Bible translations, as well as translating into English two books on the history of the biblical text published by the German Bible Society (E. Würthwein, *The Text of the Old Testament*, 1979, revised 1995; K. and B. Aland, *The Text of the New Testament*, 1987, revised 1989).

TRANSLATION CRITICISM – THE POTENTIALS AND LIMITATIONS

Categories and Criteria
for Translation Quality Assessment

By
Katharina Reiss

Translated by
Erroll F. Rhodes

AMERICAN
BIBLE
SOCIETY

St. Jerome Publishing
Manchester, UK

Published by

    St. Jerome Publishing
    2 Maple Road West, Brooklands
    Manchester, M23 9HH, United Kingdom
    Tel +44 161 973 9856 / Fax +44 161 905 3498
    stjerome@compuserve.com / http://www.mcc.ac.uk/stjerome

and

    American Bible Society
    1865 Broadway
    New York, NY 10023, United States of America
    http://www.americanbible.org

ISBN 1-900650-26-6 (St. Jerome Publishing, pbk)
ISBN 1-58516-124-1 (American Bible Society, pbk)

© St. Jerome Publishing 2000

Printed and bound in Great Britain by Biddles Ltd., Guildford, Surrey, UK

Cover design by Steve Fieldhouse, Oldham, UK (+44 161 620 2263)

Typeset by Delta Typesetters, Cairo, Egypt
Email: delttyp@starnet.com.eg

British Library Cataloguing in Publication Data
A catalogue record of this book is available from the British Library

Library of Congress Catalguing in Publication Data
A catalogue record of this book is available from the Library of Congress

Contents

Translator's Preface

It has been almost thirty years since Katharina Reiss contributed the twelfth in a series of college texts published by Max Hueber Verlag, a slim paperback entitled *Möglichkeiten und Grenzen der Übersetzungskritik*, outlining principles for assessing the quality of translations. Her pioneering presentation of the challenging possibilities and limitations of translation criticism came at a time when academic and professional leaders were becoming acutely aware of the vital significance of sharing information across cultural borders in a world constantly growing smaller. This work proved to be seminal and it remains today a classic, still valuable for anyone engaged in producing or evaluating translations.

Although the book was originally addressed to the wide spectrum of translation professionals and researchers, we believe it may be especially significant for a particular segment of this audience, namely Bible translators and Bible translation consultants. This is because Bible translators – so gifted in normative approaches to the field – may be able to profit immeasurably from the insights and approaches that characterize modern translation studies with their accent on descriptive approaches to the theory and practice of translation.

In the three decades since Katharina Reiss wrote, the terminology of translation studies has evolved on many fronts. For example, the terms "equivalence" and "fidelity" today are associated with different meanings and values. In translating Reiss's book, we have tried to be faithful to her presentation, while at the same time using terminology that today's reader would generally understand and value.

In preparing the present text for English readers certain aspects of its format have been slightly modified. For example, the number of footnotes has been reduced by about one fifth to eliminate detailed references to older ephemeral publications and dated illustrations. Further, the citation of references has been moved from footnotes to author-date insertions in the text in accordance with recent scholarly usage.

Finally, we wish to thank both Hueber Verlag and the author for kindly allowing us to translate and publish this book. We are also specially indebted to Mary Snell-Hornby for graciously reviewing the translation and contributing many valuable suggestions, as well as to the staff of the Research Center for Scripture and Media, in particular, Liza L. Young, J. Scott Dilley, Deborah G. Atkinson and Scott S. Elliott, for their painstaking work in arranging the bibliographical references and preparing the index. We hope that readers of this book will find it as useful and stimulating as did the translator.

Erroll F. Rhodes
New York, New York
Feast of St. Jerome

Foreword

About thirty years ago, when I was working as an editorial consultant at Max Hueber Publishers in Munich, I was given a manuscript
to assess on an exciting new topic: translation critique, using objective and strictly verifiable criteria, as opposed to the purely practical,
do-it-yourself methods typical of the time. The author, Katharina
Reiss, had worked for some time as a teacher of translation at the
Institute of Translation and Interpreting of the University of
Heidelberg, and she could obviously draw on many years of thought
and experience. The manuscript impressed us all as being some-
thing of great promise for the study of translation ("Translation
Studies", as we now know the subject, had not yet been identified),
and it was published in 1971 as Volume 12 in the series *Hueber
Hochschulreihe* under the title *Möglichkeiten und Grenzen der
Übersetzungskritik. Kategorien und Kriterien für eine sachgerechte
Beurteilung von Übersetzungen.*

Now, in the year 2000, Katharina Reiss's book is still selling,
and it has long since achieved the status of a pioneer work in the
discipline of Translation Studies in the German-speaking area. Her
approach must have been used in hundreds of diploma theses as the
classical model of translation critique, and her arguments provoked
heated debates in scholarly journals right into the 1990s. Reiss has
meanwhile developed her ideas, not only in her 1976 monograph
Texttyp und Übersetzungsmethode. Der operative Text, but also in
many essays and lectures, and the book she wrote with Hans J.
Vermeer, *Grundlegung einer allgemeinen Translationstheorie* (published 1984) is widely known as the basic work on functional
translation theory in Germany (*Skopostheorie*).

It is high time, it seems, for an English version of her pioneering
book, and the present initiative is more than welcome. While many
observations must be seen against the background of the late 1960s,
the model of translation critique and the thoughts that inspired it
still make stimulating reading for anyone interested in translation.

We can only hope that Katharina Reiss will be as greatly appreciated by her English-speaking readers as she has been in Germany.

Mary Snell-Hornby
Vienna, February 2000

Author's Foreword

In an age when the world is constantly growing smaller, when nations are increasingly drawn closer together and the necessity for exchanging information and ideas across borders in both oral and written forms has become a fact of life, communication has become inconceivable without translation. It is especially important in international scientific endeavors to communicate the results of research rapidly and accurately, not only so that new insights can be shared, but also for avoiding an unnecessary duplication of effort. Translators and interpreters have long been employed in international politics, and they are now increasingly present at interregional conferences of economic, industrial and scientific interests. Finally, the translation of literary works as well as of forms of amusement and entertainment play a significant role in mutual exchanges between cultures.

The sheer bulk and undeniable significance of translations in today's world require that the quality of translations be a matter of special attention. But this is not the only motivation for being concerned with principles for evaluating translations. Undeniably many poor translations have been made and even published. An interest in better translations could be stimulated by more contextually sensitive principles of criticism. From a pedagogical perspective as well the development of objective methods of evaluating, translations would have advantages, because it would be an excellent and even more attractive way of honing an awareness of language and of expanding the critic's linguistic and extralinguistic horizons. And finally, a careful study of the potential and limitations of translation criticism is all the more necessary because the present state of the art is inadequate. The standards most often observed by critics are generally arbitrary, so that their pronouncements do not reflect a solid appreciation of the translation process.

The purpose of this book is to formulate appropriate categories and objective criteria for the evaluation of all kinds of translations.

It is essential to develop a general framework that will accommodate the range of standards relevant to specific individual
translations. This leads to the recognition that different kinds of
texts call for different kinds of standards. A typology of texts to be
translated is the first step toward determining the literary, linguistic
and pragmatic categories which provide the points of reference by
which a particular translation is to be evaluated.

Once these basic questions have been clarified, the limitations
of translation criticism should be defined and categories developed
that will consistently ensure the objectivity of judgments or expose
their subjectivity.

The following pages undertake the task of proposing a work-
able and flexible framework that is sufficiently broad to include the
whole range of texts subject to translation, and yet is no more specialized or detailed than is necessary for it to be useful as a model.

A. Introduction

> Now that it is translated and finished, everybody can read
> and criticize it. One now runs his eyes over three or four
> pages and does not stumble once – without realizing what
> boulders and clods had once lain there where he now goes
> along as over a smoothly-planed board. We had to sweat
> and toil there before we got those boulders and clods out of
> the way, so that one could go along so easily. The plowing
> goes well when the field is cleared.
>
> Martin Luther (1963)

"Plowing is easy when the field is clear," Luther would say to the
critics of his translations in 1530 when they showed themselves all
too ready with their criticisms. And all the same he had the satisfac-
tion of having his translations "criticized" at all.

How has the situation changed with regard to translation criticism today? Putting the question in this way suggests that there is
such a thing as translation criticism. But is there? Of course, in one
place or another translations have always been discussed, evaluated
and criticized. Daily and weekly periodicals, as well as quarterlies
and annuals feature, reviews and discussions of translations. But
do these represent translation criticism in the strict sense?

It has been remarked often enough that with the advent of com-
mercialization in the literary world, the level of literary criticism
(apart from some outstanding exceptions) has generally sunk alarm-
ingly low. The criticism of literary *translations* in no way constitutes
an exception.[1] And yet the simple fact that every year more than
three thousand books are translated into German, not to mention
the technical translations, essays, speeches and reports that are
churned out daily by hosts of translators, might make one think that

---

[1] The passionate arguments over translations of the world's literary classics in
the Romantic period come to mind, with their attempts to form a theoretical
analysis of the problem of translation.

greater attention would be devoted by literary critics to translation criticism. But no such tendency has been observed. Apart from
a few exceptions (Schneider, 1956), which are as sparse as the
knowledge of their original languages is restricted, reviews of translations do not usually judge them as translations at all. And when
they do, it is usually only in passing and with such trite phrases as
"translated fluently," "reads like an original," "excellent translation," or "sensitively translated" – judgments that are almost always
vague and unsupported. Reviewers rarely take the time and effort
to compare a translation with its original language version, even if
they are familiar with the language. It will happen more frequently
if the language of the original is either English or French, less frequently if it is another European language, and very rarely if it is
any other language. The result is outrageous: a work is examined
for its content, style and sometimes also for its esthetic character,
and both the author and his work are judged only on the basis of a
translation without consulting the original work. This fact itself is
usually assumed tacitly, with neither positive nor negative mention.
The author is judged solely by proxy, via the translator, in absentia
and without the fact even being mentioned.[2]

There is, of course, the question whether judging a translation
lies within the competence of a literary critic. Is a critic's knowledge of the literature or degree of specialization in a given field an
adequate qualification for the task? Does he have a sound appreciation of the boulders and clods (to use Luther's phrase) that the
translator first had to clear away? Can he distinguish something
other than the final product of the translation process, which then is
treated as an original?

In the light of these considerations we may conclude that translation criticism is possible only by persons who are familiar with

---

[2] On rare occasions a reviewer may show an awareness of this fact. Thus M.
Reich-Ranicki (1965, p. 72) writes: "Hemingway's style has had an influence
on a whole generation of German writers. But whose style has actually had this
influence? Hemingway's, or that of Annemarie Horschitz-Horst, his translator?"

both the target and source languages,[3] and is accordingly in a position to compare the translation directly with its original. In brief, translation criticism requires a comparison of the target and source texts.

Translation criticism (although under different names) is practiced more consistently and intensively in translator training institutions than in publishing houses. The students' practical translation exercises and their examinations, whether on the elementary or more advanced levels, are "corrected" and graded, i.e., criticized and evaluated. Here again we may ask whether the correctors give sufficient attention to the range of possibilities offered, expected, or even desired. What criteria are employed beyond the obvious ones of vocabulary blunders and misunderstood grammatical constructions? To what extent does the corrector simply rely on his own feelings? The same questions are relevant for the revisor and the evaluator. They all need to set the translation beside the original and compare the two together. But do any objective points of reference or guidelines for evaluating a work of translation exist?

Every translation project is a balancing process achieved by constructing a target text under the constant restraint of a source text. While trying to find the closest equivalents in the target language, the translator must always have one eye on the source text in order to confirm the adequacy of the equivalents (Kade, 1964, p. 137).[4]

---

[3] The terms *source language* and *target language* (German: Ausgangssprache, Zielsprache; French: langue de depart, langue d'arrivée) for the language of the original and the language of the translation are now so universally accepted in the literature of translation that they are adopted here as standard terms. Only for stylistic reasons are such alternatives used as *the language of the original* (or *of the author*) for the source language, or *the language of the translation* for the target language.

[4] For the science of translating the term *equivalence* is a core concept. Equivalence may obtain both between the totality of the original text and its version in the target language, and between the individual elements in the text and its translation. Equivalence is not simply correspondence, nor is it reproduction of the original language unit. Equivalence is, as its etymology suggests, "equal value," i.e., corresponding target language expressions may be considered optimally equivalent if they represent the linguistic and circumstantial context, the usage

The specific individual translation, the result of this process, should be evaluated by objective and relevant criteria. Only then is it possible for the more or less spontaneous practice of translation criticism to meet the benchmark of an objective translation critique.

What is meant by *objective* translation criticism? In the present context objectivity means to be verifiable as in contrast to arbitrary and inadequate. This means that every criticism of a translation, whether positive or negative, must be defined explicitly and be verified by examples. The critic should also always make allowance for other subjective options. In a negative criticism the critic should try to ascertain what led the translator to make the (alleged) error. On the one hand this process opens an opportunity for examining the background of the passage, of placing it in a broader context, and determining possible causes of the error, whether these may be carelessness or a typographical oversight in the source or target language, inexperience in the idiom or technical terminology of a field, inadequate sensitivity to matters of style in the target language, insufficient familiarity with the medium (radio, television, theater), etc., which would affect the seriousness of the misjudgment in the light of the entire context. On the other hand it can be beneficial for the critic, sometimes revealing an insight that was overlooked in an initial adverse judgment. In any event, the critic's reader is given the opportunity of considering two different judgments and of weighing their respective probability and value afresh.

But then this also raises the challenge of matching any negative criticism with a suggestion for an improvement. According to Lessing, "a reviewer need not be able to improve on what he criticizes," but he also comments that "the art critic does not simply recognize that something disturbs him, but he goes on to say 'because ...' And, of course, if this 'because' is a well considered 'because,' it naturally leads further to a statement of how the offending element should have been handled so that it would not have

---

and level of style, and the intention of the author in the target language which carry the same value as the expressions in the source language. See the discussion of potential and optimal equivalents below (§3).

been disturbing" (Lessing, n.d., p. 68). And A. W. von Schlegel (1963, p. 99) himself an experienced and successful translator, made the comment that "It seems to me a very reasonable demand that when translations are criticized there should always be a proposed remedy." To avoid any suspicion of mere quibbling, this principle should always be observed.

If objectivity is to be matched with *relevant* criteria and categories in translation criticism, care must be taken to recognize that the text being evaluated is a *translation*, and is discussed *as such*. Consequently such matters as the author's literary quality, imaginativeness, intellectual profundity, scholarly precision, etc., are of less concern than determining objectively (i.e., verifiably) whether and to what extent the text in the target language represents the content of the text in the source language.

Here again in regard to *constructive* translation criticism there is the challenge of offering counterproposals for rejected solutions. A comparison with the original offers the critic's reader an opportunity of choosing between different equivalents. Walter Widmer (1959, p. 82) offers an instructive example of this. Widmer censures a translator for a poor translation of the French expression "une abondance de gestes." He calls this expression of Flaubert's an example of "vague words for vague thoughts," and from a review of the various German translations available he concludes that "the translator (justifiably) understood as little by it as did Flaubert." But then, in this the translator is being precisely appropriate. It is not his duty to compensate for the author and invent some particular gesture or gestures that the context might seem to warrant, i.e., as the critic Widmer proposes, to replace "une abondance de gestes" with what he considers "a better translation": "incessantly shrugging his shoulders and shaking his head." The critic's reader is not going to be convinced by this reasoning and will side with the maligned translator. Quite apart from the fact that Widmer's proposal raises other objections (it may suggest that the man has a nervous tic), it simply does not correspond to the lack in the original text of any explicit description of the gestures, whether this was intentional or not.

Now since we are discussing texts, we should pause to note briefly the relation of this basic concept to *translation*. It has been popular among philologists (Friedrich, 1968, p 5; Kloepfer, 1967, p. 10; Schadewaldt, 1963, p. 252) since the days of Schleiermacher (1963, p. 62) to draw a distinction between "interpreting" (non-literary texts[5]) and translating (literary texts). Incidentally, this distinction is given formal expression by Hans-Joachim Störig (1963, p. 15) in the preface to his anthology: "The *oral* process of interpreting is distinguished from the *written* process of translating: the act of the interpreter (unless recorded in minutes or on tape) is fleeting and transitory, while that of the translator is fixed and permanent." When we speak of translation criticism in the following pages, we do not use the term in the broad sense which includes every communication from one language into another, but rather in the (commonplace) sense of *written translation of a fixed written text* "from one natural language into another" (Delavenay, 1960, p. 13).

Anthony G. Oettinger (1963, p. 449) remarked in his book: "No matter how difficult it may be to translate, it is even more difficult to judge a translation. Everyone works on his own." Undoubtedly there can be objective criteria for making a relevant evaluation of a translation, but they have not yet been adequately recognized or systematically established and described. Subjective and objective criteria for judging translations have become so arbitrary that the lines between literary criticism and translation criticism are completely blurred. Reviews that are purportedly objective, representing translation criticism in the strict sense, all too often lack any defined points of reference, overarching integrity, or pertinent categories, so that the final result is an impression of complete arbitrariness.

One of the causes for the inadequacies of translation criticism to date may be traced to the wide variety of views as to what a transla-

---

[5] The German term "dolmetschen" is used of unwritten oral or simultaneous translation, in contrast to "übersetzen" which refers to written translations that are subject to subsequent examination or verification. (Tr.)

tion can or should achieve, or even the doubt as to whether translation is in fact at all possible.[6] A theory of translation that is applicable
to *all* texts has not yet been developed. The last fifteen years, however, have seen an interesting series of attempts to address the topic.
The following deserve special notice: Otto Kade (1964), Rudolf
Walter Jumpelt (1961), Eugene A. Nida (1964), Rolf Kloepfer
(1967) and Ralph-Rainer Wuthenow (1969). Kade's work is concerned expressly with "pragmatic" texts, while Jumpelt is interested
primarily in translating technical scientific texts. Nida deals with
problems of Bible translation. Kloepfer focuses exclusively on "literary" texts including both prose and poetical compositions, and
Wuthenow concentrates on the specific problems in translating literary classics.

Apart from the ways in which the respective kinds of text are
distinguished or defined, the works just mentioned also suggest the
dangers of extrapolating from their findings, i.e., applying their conclusions to *all* texts. In retrospect it may appear better to proceed
from the general to the particular, as the present work attempts to
do. And yet it is absolutely necessary to keep attention constantly
centered on the question of translation because, as we have noted,
the legitimate demands that can and must be made on a translation
have not been effectively formulated, and the criteria and categories for critical evaluation cannot be formulated without a systematic
account of the requirements, the presuppositions and the goals, of
every translation process.[7]

---

[6] See J. Ortega y Gasset (1937). But *contra*, see G. Mounin (1967, p. 111):
"Translation is neither totally and for ever impossible, nor totally and forever
possible;" and p. 112, "If an expression actually cannot be translated, a translator in the twentieth century is at least capable of knowing and understanding
why the expression cannot be translated." See also J. C. Catford (1965, p. 93),
"Source language texts and items are 'more' or 'less' translatable rather than
absolutely 'translatable' or 'untranslatable'."
[7] See H. Friedrich (1969, p. 7): "For in contrast to the other linguistic arts, in
the art of translating and reviewing translations we cannot do without structural
standards, and especially the standards which have been developed from the late
eighteenth century to the present in significant statements on translations."

These observations are programmatic for the following chapters. The theoretical consideration of translating and translation criticism will be supported by a critical evaluation of the available literature on the subject. Theoretical explanations will be fully illustrated by examples.[8] The examples given are not my own, but taken as far as possible from original texts and published translations. Since the examples are shown without their contexts, the equivalents given make no claim to be the best; it should be obvious that in different linguistic situations and circumstances other equivalents would be as valid. When it is particularly useful or when central problems are involved, special aspects of the procedures followed by translation critics will be reviewed. In this way the reader with purely practical interests may find something useful and instructive.

---

[8] Illustrative examples throughout will be taken from the main European languages of English, French and Spanish. Beyond this the following discussion lays no claim to universal validity. How far the principles developed are relevant to non-European languages remains an open question. The attempt is merely to propose for discussion one of several possible methodological models.

B. The Potential of Translation Criticism

> Nothing is more difficult than to enter into the thought processes of another person and be able to rebuild his whole perspective in all its particularity .... And yet it is only when one can reconstruct the framework and how it operates in all its parts that one can claim to understand a work and its spirit. Formulating this general understanding in explicit terms is called characterizing, and this constitutes the task and essence of criticism.
>
> Friedrich Schlegel, 1804

Schlegel's statement about the essence of criticism goes doubly for translation criticism. Doubly, because for the critic to make a properly balanced judgment on a translation, not only must the translator's work be characterized, but it must also constantly be compared with the original "in all its particularity," making a "general understanding" of the original author's work the touchstone authenticating any final judgment. This consideration underlies the maxim we stressed in the Introduction as a basic requirement: No critique without a comparison with the original! This process of comparison is indispensable for a balanced judgment; any alternative would only invite charges of subjectivity and caprice.

1. Criticism and the target language text

And yet the widespread traditional practice of limiting criticism to translated texts may have a degree of justification, at least for literary texts. This kind of criticism, based solely on the translation in the target language with no consideration for the original, can be useful only if its inherent limitations are acknowledged. What lies within the range of these limitations?

The judgment of a translation should never be made *one-sidedly* and *exclusively* on the basis of its form in the target language. If the work is a novel, the translation critic may well assume it to be an

example of light fiction, while in actual fact the translator has simply been incapable of integrating the text's elements of content,
structure and style.[9] A definitive judgment is possible only if its
inadequacies can also be observed and demonstrated in the source
of the translation. It should be evident that the analysis and evaluation of a translated text can serve as the first stage, but it must be
followed by the second and indispensable stage of comparison with
the source text.

In some instances, of course, the reverse process is also possible, as when comparing several translations from a single original.
Horst von Tscharner (1963) gives an example of such an approach.
Tscharner first gives an analysis of a poem in its original form, and
then proceeds to exhibit several translations together with his comments for and against their solutions.

But usually the first step begins with the translated text. How,
then, should the critic begin?

As Julius Wirl (1958, p. 64) states, "A person who cannot read
the original may not be able to use the same criteria as one who can,
but other criteria may be available. A novel in translation may be
judged by certain values that are expected of the category, and the
translation adjudged so fluent that it does not read like a translation." But there are further questions which must also be considered:
1. whether the original was written in a fluent style so that the fluency of the translation corresponds to it; and 2. whether fluency in
a translation is an absolute or a relative value, i.e., whether fluency
is a necessary characteristic, something to be striven for in every
kind of text under all circumstances, or even a universally desirable
goal for a translation. These questions will be discussed more thoroughly elsewhere.[10]

---

[9] See H. F. Foltin (1968, p. 267): "This brings us to what for literary studies is
probably the essential characteristic of inferior forms of *belles lettres*, namely
how far they fail to integrate the elements of content, structure and style which
are dependent on the constant and variable factors described above, ... for it is
the combination of these elements that determines esthetic quality for the literary scholar. At the lowest level of quality we encounter innumerable errors
of fact, composition and style that reflect the author's ineptitude; ..."

[10] See 6.1 (Resumés and summaries) and 6.7 (Scholarly translations).

It is generally acknowledged today that a translator should have "a real talent for writing in his own language" (Sir Stanley Unwin, in *On Translation*: See Güttinger [1963, p. 219]) since "clumsiness in the language of the translation has a certain prejudicial effect on the work as a whole," because "if a translator does not have a mastery of his own language and is incapable of writing well, his translation is bound to be poor, however well he may understand the text" (Hillaire Belloc: See Güttinger [1963, p. 219]). Hans Erich Nossack (1965, p. 12) puts it even more strongly when he insists: "the purpose is to place in the hands of the reader a readable book in the reader's own language, and not some schoolboy's raw gloss, reproducing sentence structures, participial constructions and the like, whether Anglicisms, Latinisms, or whatever. An awkward and artificial translation can do more to kill a foreign masterpiece than a smattering of outright errors in translation."

Awkward and artificial expressions in the target language can certainly be identified without reference to the original text. According to Fritz Güttinger (1963, p. 143ff) a rough gauge of a [German] translation can be gained by a simple spot-check: "Just think of the words that occur most frequently in German and do not occur in the foreign language, and you can tell whether a translation is any good. In a word-for-word translation these words will be lacking because they are not in the original. The missing words tell whether the translator really knows German and can meet the first requirement for making a good translation."

This practical rule of thumb (which has its limitations, as do all such rules) can apply not only to "words that occur most frequently in German and do not occur in the foreign language," but also to all the concepts and idioms that are expressed differently in the foreign language. If the critic is very knowledgeable in the source language, he will easily recognize instances in the target language where the translator has slipped up. Slips and oversights of this kind can cast a cloud on the quality of a translation.

This is illustrated by the account in the *Süddeutschen Zeitung* for April 22, 1970, given by the Spanish news correspondent M. von Conta of his interview with the then Spanish Foreign Minister,

Gregorio López Bravo. He reported: "López: Der Handel zwischen unsern Ländern, bei dem zum Ausdruck kommt, daß die deutsche Bundesrepublik einen Vorzugsplatz unter *unsern Käufern und Verkäufern* einnimmt ...." ["López: Trade between our countries may be characterized by the fact that the Federal Republic of Germany occupies a special place among our *buyers and sellers*"]. This rendering of the Minister's response not only sounds odd in German ("unsere Verkäufer," *our sellers* could be misunderstood), it is also grammatically wrong. The German word "Handelspartner" (*trading partners*), for which Spanish lacks a single word, did not occur to the reporter. The concept is usually expressed in Spanish by "compradores y suministradores" (= "Käufer und Lieferanten" *buyers and suppliers*); the literal translation in place of the idiomatic "Handelspartner" (*trading partners*) reflects an inadequate command of the language.

Another example: "Die natürliche Logik enthält zwei Fehler: Sie sieht nicht, daß die Sprachphänomene für den Sprechenden weithin Hintergrundscharakter haben und mithin außerhalb seines kritischen Bewußtseins und seiner Kontrolle bleiben" ["This simple logic has two flaws: it does not recognize that for the speaker of a language its phenomena are largely a matter of background, and consequently lie beyond the range of his critical awareness and control"]. Anyone with a knowledge of English would recognize the German text as a translation from an English or American source, because the English word "control" has the meaning "exercise authority over" or "manipulate," while the German word "Kontrolle" is properly used only in the sense of "verification" or "checking". Wolf Friedrich (1969, p. 37) cites this example and comments: "It is wrong and misleading. People can *verify* the phenomena of a language, but not *manipulate* them – this is not in their power."

The translator's knowledge of a language is not to be gauged simply by the criteria of words lacking in the vocabulary of the source language, or by the recognition of *false friends*, but even more by what we may call *supplemental words,* Porzig (1962, p. 145). Even Luther had to deal with this problem. Luther (1963, p. 20f) defended his method of translating Romans 3, where the Latin does not have the word *solum* and he introduced the word "allein" (*alone*) in his German translation: "But it is the nature of our German language that in speaking of two things, one of which is affirmed and the other denied, we use the word solum 'allein' [*alone* or *only*] along with the word *nicht* [*not*] or *kein* [*no*] .... It is the nature of the German language to add the word *allein* in order that the word *nicht* or *kein* may be clearer and more complete." This "allein" which Luther defends is an example of supplemental words, particles which do not serve in German as relational connectives but define the nature of a sentence (a speech-act). In many other languages there are no lexical forms which correspond to these particles (such as eben, etwa, doch, nur, aber, auch, überhaupt, etc.) in their distinctive, intensive or clarifying function.[11] In Spanish and English these nuances can only be inferred from the entire context, and then not always with certainty, so that any translation necessarily involves a degree of subjective interpretation. This is especially true of written texts where the aid of intonation which would clarify the intention of the spoken word is lacking. Especially in texts where the translation must not only be in correct but also fluent and idiomatic German, it is appropriate to make use of these particles, even when there is nothing in the literal text of the source that would correspond to them.[12]

When translating from German to Spanish or English, on the other hand, it is necessary to consider carefully whether these particles

---

[11] In German they serve to add a certain nuance to a question, an exclamation, a request, or a statement. In a question they may imply the *expected* answer: "Soll ich das *etwa* glauben?" ["Should I *ever* believe that?"] suggesting the answer "No." They may add emphasis to a request or exclamation: "Das ist *doch* nicht möglich!" ["That is *just* impossible!"] which contrasts with the simple "Das ist nicht möglich!" by a degree of personal emphasis. See W. Porzig (1962, p. 145 f.).

[12] Accordingly H. J. Kann considers the introduction of these "necessary" words in a German translation as altogether commendable. See Kann (1968, p. 57): "This subtle distinction between the two languages [conservative formal English and a more aggressive German] is made particularly noticeable by the large number of words which are necessarily added in German to flesh out the implications and emphases of the text." Similarly pp. 84-85 and 114.

carry full weight in the sentence, or only serve it with an element of nuance. The decision then has to be made whether to translate them with equivalent expressions, or to ignore them (representing them by a null equivalent).[13]

This suggests another criterion for judging a translation solely on the basis of its target language: a mastery of stylistic and grammatical standards must be supported by a familiarity with idiomatic usage.

And there is yet another way of evaluating a translated text: internal inconsistencies. H. Kellner (1964, p. 87) writes: "Absurdities may be conspicuous even without a comparison of the two texts, for which most critics do not take the time." These "absurdities" might be simple translation errors due to an inadequate knowledge of the vocabulary or grammar of the source language, or even a failure to appreciate non-verbal factors[14] operative in the target language, though this requires a comparison with the source language for confirmation. Errors of this kind generally occur on the semantic level of translation, bringing to the lexical, grammatical and stylistic criteria a fourth and last criterion which can be relevant to judging the target language version of a text.

As we have noted, a critique based on the target language version of a text can be quite productive. But our discussion has indicated that on the whole its role in the evaluation of a translation is distinctly limited. It is limited by a lack of reference to the original, and if it is to avoid such vague generalities as "fluent translation," "reads like an original,"[15] "uneven translation," etc., it needs to be

---

[13] In the sentence "Ich habe dieses Buch *auch* gelesen" the word *auch* is significant: in Spanish it would be "Yo *también* he leído el libro," and in English "I have read this book, *too*." In the sentence "Hast du auch *gelesen*, was du unterschreibst?" the *auch* is a nuance word. Translating it by *también* or *too* would distort the meaning of the German word, so that the translation should be "¿Has leído lo que estás firmando?" or "Have you read what you are signing?"

[14] See the discussion of non-verbal factors below (B.4).

[15] See A. Luther (1949, p. 11), "The highest praise bestowed on a translation is generally that it reads like an original. But is that really a high form of praise?" And further on he comments on a translation of Tolstoy, "I compared the translation with the original and found that the translator has dissolved Tolstoy's

supplemented by a close comparison with the original. Besides, an evaluation on the basis of the translation alone has a largely negative cast. Conformity to grammatical and stylistic standards as well as lexical and semantic norms of the target language are only to be expected, or at least should be, and should warrant no particular conclusions. It can only call attention to any deviations from standard usage.

Our first principle, that translation criticism should be constructive, would rule out judging a translation solely on the basis of its faults. Hans Erich Nossack (1965, p. 11), who is no mean critic, was quite representative in saying: "I frankly confess that as a reader I would rather put up with a few insignificant errors in a translation, which I probably wouldn't notice anyway, than with a betrayal of the whole spirit of a book which could not be ignored and which would make it a lifeless and tedious piece of work."

However much we may welcome this generosity of the critic toward translation errors (provided they are few), the parallel emphasis on the positive quality of a translation, or its consistency with "the overall spirit of the book," should not be determined on the basis of a subjective impression ("a lifeless piece of work"). For this a comparison with its original is essential, and judgments must be based on strict and objective criteria.

Furthermore, as we noted at the beginning, it goes without saying that constructive translation criticism must also offer satisfactory alternative translations, substantiated with convincing evidence. Since success in dealing with translation problems can be determined only by a comparison with the text in the original language, reference to the original text provides the only effective means for establishing a detailed evaluation of a translation.

2. Criticism and the source language text

The discussion thus far has made it clear that the evaluation of a

---

lengthy periods into sequences of brief sentences .... The translation does read like *an* original, but it does not read like *the* original."

translation solely on the basis of the target language can be valuable for strictly limited purposes. But a conclusive evaluation cannot be made without comparing the translation with the original. One of the most important principles for translators is complete fidelity to the intent of the original author. Only by a comparison with the source language can it be discovered whether this fidelity has been achieved, how well the intent of the author has been understood, how it has been interpreted, and how successfully it has been expressed in the target language. Evaluation on the basis of the source language represents criticism which takes this fact into account.

Before an *overall* evaluation of a translation can be made, it must be examined from a variety of perspectives. In other words, criticism should begin with observing the type of text represented, which has significant implications for a valid translation, and then consider both the linguistic and non-linguistic factors which are of essential significance for the translation process. It is necessary for an objective and relevant evaluation to consider the characteristics of each *type of text*, its *linguistic elements* and the *non-linguistic factors* affecting the linguistic form of the original. The following pages will discuss the basic steps toward a clear assessment of the factors involved in constructing objective criteria and relevant categories for translation criticism.

2.1 Text types and translation methods

Just as the translator must realize what kind of text he is translating before he begins working with it, the critic must also be clear as to the kind of text represented by the original if he is to avoid using inappropriate standards to judge the translation.

For example, it would be a mistake to use the same criteria in judging pulp fiction and serious literature, or opera librettos and patent specifications. Yet this obvious principle has hardly been observed with any notable consistency.

A typology of texts that is sensitive to the necessities of the translation process and also includes all the varieties of text that are encountered is accordingly a non-negotiable prerequisite for any objective approach to translation criticism. The literature is replete with various attempts to develop a typology based on principles of translation and translation techniques. These attest to a recognition that translation methods should not be determined solely by the particular target audience or special purpose intended for the translation (as so often suggested). The influence of both these factors will be discussed in the chapters on the limitations of translation criticism. But first it is important to examine normal examples of translation, where the purpose is to transfer the text of the original into a second language without abridgment, expansion or any particular spin, representing the source text with corresponding text in the target language. In this kind of normal situation it is the type of text which decides the approach for the translator; the type of text is the primary factor influencing the translator's choice of a proper translation method.

Theoretical considerations of the problem of translation have always drawn a fundamental distinction between pragmatic and literary translations, although this distinction has been drawn (unfortunately) in such a way that pragmatic translations were seen as more or less free of problems and therefore not deserving any detailed attention,[16] while for the translation of literary works the greatest variety of theories were developed, refined, debated and defended. This distinction is certainly quite valid, and has been widely accepted. Even W. E. Süskind (1959, p. 85) uses it when he insists that translators of literary works must themselves be talented creative writers, in contrast to translators of practical works whom he calls specialist translators. This can be accepted without

---

[16] See the treatment in F. Schleiermacher (1963, p. 38 ff., especially pp. 40-45). Actually it is useless to posit a graded order of texts, whether by their degree of difficulty or dignity, as it is generally done following Schleiermacher. All kinds of practical texts are relegated to the lowest level, with literary prose far above them, and with metrical prose and poetry, especially lyric poetry at the highest level of difficulty. Yet despite this common assessment a complex contract (cf. L. Weisgerber, 1961) can sometimes present far greater difficulties than the average novel, and a translator with a poetical bent will have far less difficulty translating a lyrical poem than translating a technical manual.

reservation, because language for practical texts is primarily a means of communication, of conveying information, while for literary prose and poetry it is a tool of artistic creativity, conveying esthetic values.[17]

This rough division, however, is completely inadequate because both groups contain multiple varieties of texts presenting quite different problems, each requiring a different translation approach based on different principles. Practical texts may share a wide variety of characteristics, but it still makes a great difference whether the translation to be evaluated is a commercial inventory, a legal brief, or a philosophical treatise. On the other hand, the common factors in literary translations are matched by a wide range of different perspectives: Translations of sophisticated essays and lyrical poetry are not to be judged by the same standards. Translations of stage plays require attention to many details that can quite happily be ignored in other kinds of literary translations.

In recent decades the importance of this basic insight has increasingly come to be recognized, and yet the various attempts that have been made to identify the characteristics of different kinds of text have been plagued by a peculiar lack of lucidity.

Elsa Tabernig de Pucciarelli (1964, p. 144ff) presents a threefold analysis in her essay "Aspectos técnicos y literarios de la traducción": 1. technical scientific texts, where characteristically a knowledge of technical facts takes precedence over linguistic proficiency, and the latter is required to cover the special terminology of special fields; 2. philosophical texts, where the intellectual ability of the translator to grasp intuitively the dimensions of the author's conceptual world is more important than the details of terminology; and 3. literary texts, where not only matters of content, but also of artistic form must be mastered and recreated in the target language.

But this three-fold analyasis is also unsatisfactory. The justification for "philosophical texts" as an additional type is not convincingly demonstrated. Particularly the assumption that the

---

[17] The use of language in the first instance may be characterized as mainly denotative, and in the second as mainly connotative.

translator must master the terminology of philosophy in no way constitutes a distinctive criterion in comparison with other fields. Nor
does the requirement of a sympathetic grasp of an author's conceptual world add anything to the universally valid principle that
understanding precedes translating.

As a second example from the Hispanic world we may take
Francisco Ayala (1965, p. 23ff). He also recognizes the necessity to
distinguish different kinds of text, especially in regard to various
translation methods: "Since a written culture encompasses an end-
less variety of texts which require for translation the versatile
application of various and constantly adaptive solutions to the problems they present case by case, a mathematical treatise, a political
discourse, a comedy and a lyrical poem cannot all be translated in
the same way."[18] It should be noted positively that Ayala duly
acknowledges the variety of practical texts, yet in the end his observations revert to the usual dichotomy, and despite excellent
individual insights, the result remains confused.

Another three-fold analysis of textual types is found in Peter
Brang's (1963, p. 421ff) essay. Brang reviews the work of A.
Fedorov, one of the early leading translation scholars of the So-
viet Union. Basing his analysis on the various types of translation
material, he distinguished: 1. news and reviews, business and official documents, and scientific texts; 2. organizational and political
documents (including the works of classical Marxists, editorials and
speeches); and 3. literary texts.

The general characteristic of the first group[19] is described as
the presence of specialized technical terms and expressions.[20] The

---

[18] "Pues la incalculable variedad de textos en que se concreta una cultura escrita
ha de requerir una aplicación alternativa y siempre cambiante de las soluciones
diversas al problema que su traducción plantea en cada caso: no pueden
traducirse de igual manera un tratado matemático, un discurso político, una
comedia, un poema lírico."

[19] The present discussion of Fedorov's analysis is based solely on P. Brang's
essay, because the Russian original was not available.

[20] Examples of these expressions are: "Based on this evidence we conclude ..."
(scientific texts), "Informed sources report that ..." (news), "With reference to
your letter of [date] ..." (business), etc.

greatest requirement for an adequate translation is that the translator observe the literal syntax of the original with the least possible personal intrusion or deviation.

This requirement is reasonable enough provided the text is not the statement of a particular author who is responsible not only for the "what" (content) but also the "how" (manner) of its expression. A mastery of the sophisticated *terminology* of a field is essential, however, (although this aspect is hardly mentioned) if a translated text is to be at all acceptable and not strike the reader as odd, or at least as amateurish.

Fedorov sees the general characteristic of the second group, of organizational and political texts, in their mingling of scientific usages (such as technical terminology) with literary usages (such as rhetorical figures, metaphors, etc.) – overlooking the fact that this same combination of traits is found in novels and stage plays. Fedorov commends here an observance of syntactical peculiarities to preserve the rhythm of the original, especially when rendering speeches.[21] The classical Marxists writings are mentioned as pertinent examples.

The isolation of this group seems in no way justified. Either organizational and political texts belong to the pragmatic type, assuming their primary purpose is to communicate information, or they belong among literary texts, making use of rhetorical tools to achieve a particular effect which should be preserved also in a translation. Fedorov fails to make a convincing case for an organizational and political group to parallel the first and third groups. This second group does not constitute an independent type of text, but rather a mixed type resulting from the overlapping of different types, which can always happen anywhere.

Finally Fedorov characterizes the third group, literary works, as marked by a variety of stylistic and syntactic elements (dialects, professionalisms, archaisms, exotic terms) as well as a free use of

---

[21] The necessity for observing distinctions carefully, especially in rhetorical texts, will be discussed later. See section 2.2.3.

colloquialisms. But apart from the fact that this description could equally well apply to other kinds of texts which would not normally be regarded as literary, such as news reports, it seems too one-sided and peripheral, especially as it does not touch on such significant points as the predominantly esthetic perspective in the composition of the original texts and the necessity for preserving this esthetic quality when translating. Furthermore, literary prose, dramatic works and lyric poetry are all lumped together although they each have their own particular characteristics which would justify their classification as distinct types.

Otto Kade (1964, p. 62) also sees the possibility of distinguishing a broad spectrum of different textual "types"[22] based on the content, purpose and form of a text. He emphasizes that due to the very different character of various types of text the conclusion must inevitably follow that there is no single translation pattern or model that can be equally valid for them all. Then after he has dealt with the usual distinction between pragmatic prosaic texts on the one hand and literary texts (both prose and poetry) on the other, Kade proceeds just as R. W. Jumpelt did before him (1961, pp. 24-26) to consider further subdivisions. J. B. Casagrande, an American linguist, had proposed the following groups: 1. pragmatic, 2. esthetic-artistic, 3. linguistic, and 4. ethnographic translations. Kade and also Jumpelt agree with this suggestion, although identifying the last two groups is hardly useful. Another proposal of subdivisions mentioned by both Kade and Jumpelt is that of Karl Thieme, whose essay distinguished four "ideal types" representing religious, literary, official and commercial forms of language, each adapted for different groups of people and each translated differently.[23] After mentioning these

---

[22] O. Kade's term "Textgattungen" is rather unfortunate because it suggests an equivalence to the various literary typologies, which tends to confuse rather than facilitate the development of a textual typology relevant to the field of translating, as will later be demonstrated.

[23] This classification is dismissed by R. Jumpelt as only of historical interest at most, although it presents the sole beginnings for an objective labeling of texts, i.e., by the language, the "material" of every text.

two proposed classifications Kade finally reverts to the discussion of translation problems solely in terms of pragmatic texts. Jumpelt, however, expands Casagrande's system with a very detailed but quite unsatisfactory typology of translations, to use Kade's term.[24] It is unsatisfactory not just because it lacks any basis for identifying the various "types." It goes into far too great detail for the major group of "pragmatic texts" (Jumpelt exhibits a special interest in technical and natural scientific translations in his work), while "esthetic (artistic) texts" are treated summarily. The overly detailed subdivisions of the pragmatic texts are surprising in view of the explicit demand that "every statement about the question of translating must be examined to determine whether it is merely a particular example of a translation technique," with the explicit warning against "developing special categories for characteristics in a particular type which will also be found in other types" (Kade, 1964, p. 26).

Georges Mounin (1967, pp. 113-159) has advanced the latest and most penetrating proposal yet of a classification system for translations. And yet it also lacks internal consistency. His first group, religious translations, is defined by content; the second group, literary translations, by language; the third group, poetry, by form; the fourth group, children's literature, by audience; the fifth group, translations for the stage, by its medium of presentation; the sixth group, translations for cinema, by special technical conditions; and the seventh group, technical translations, again by content.

This analysis enumerates a broad variety of different *kinds* of text, but as an analysis of different *types* of text it seems too heterogeneous and diffuse.

In the present review of representative attempts to discern in the teeming variety of texts a pattern from which conclusions for a methodology and approach to translating could be derived, two things have become quite clear. First, it cannot be denied that the type of text plays a primary role in the selection of criteria for translating,

---

[24] It is possible that O. Kade borrowed the term "textual types" from Jumpelt, although it cannot be proven.

and correspondingly also for translation criticism. Consequently it is not only justifiable but also imperative to develop a typology of texts to meet the demands of both translating and objective translation criticism. Second, the classifications thus far advanced have been inadequate, primarily because they have shown no consistent principles in defining the various types of text, and the reasons given for the distinctions that are drawn (if given at all) have been variable and weak.

Discussions about the choice of a translation method (and not only are discussions of methodologically appropriate criteria quite rare, they are never a matter of primary focus)[25] have traditionally and even recently, especially under the influence of Schleiermacher (1963, p. 47),[26] always been concerned essentially with the distinction between "literal" and "free" translations, without ever defining the reasonable extent of literalism or the limits of freedom. Even Ernst Merian-Genast (1958), who refers to Schleiermacher as frequently as does Ortega y Gasset and is also typically concerned solely with the problems of literary translation, recognizes only these two methods. He writes: "[The translator] trans-lates, i.e., he 'carries over,' and this implies two directions: either he takes the foreign author to the native reader, or he brings the native reader to the foreign author. This suggests two completely different methods of translating. In the first instance the translator conceives his task as one of so adapting the original text to the thought and speech patterns of his countrymen that they hear the foreign author speaking to them in their own language. In the second instance the reader will feel that a foreigner is speaking to him: he has to learn new ideas and expressions that are not familiar to him, and instead of being at home, he is a foreigner in a strange land." Opting for one method or the other can open the floodgates for arbitrary action. Merian-Genast shares with many other authors the view that a whole

---

[25] Even G. Feidel (1970) one of the latest German publications about translating, is quite disappointing despite its promising title.

[26] "The translator either sides with the author against the reader (= literal translation), or sides with the reader against the author (= free translation)."

range of things depend on the choice of a method. "First there is
the goal to be pursued, whether there should be greater concern for
the content or for the form of the original, and then the nature of
the language into which the translation is made, the degree of its
flexibility, its ability to welcome foreign expressions, and especially the spirit of the culture and the period it belongs to, whether
it should be self-conscious, exclusive or open-minded" (p. 25). These
statements would undoubtedly be of historical value if such considerations had determined almost exclusively the translation methods
long observed especially for so-called literary translations. With
certain strict qualifications they are still important today,[27] although
they are no longer recognized as valid in the exclusive sense described above.

A rigid either/or approach to translation methods is neither objective nor practical. A translation method should be rather fully
adapted to a text type. Naturally the definition of a text's type should
begin with the individual text, assigning it to the particular type for
which there are appropriate translation methods best designed to
preserve in translation the essential characteristics of the text. Deviations from this procedure to serve special purposes or for a special
group of readers will be considered later in detail. But such deviations have nothing to do with normal processes of translating, but
rather with other aspects of conveying the content of document from
a source language into a target language.

2.2 A text typology for translators

The debate over classifying texts for translation has clearly demonstrated that both the translators and their critics must have the same
analytical base. And this is most likely to be found in the medium
of the texts themselves: *language*. Since texts require the medium
of language for their expression (although mathematical formulae
may not require translation), each text must be examined to deter-

---

[27] See the discussions in sections 6 and 7.

mine precisely what function of language it represents. According to Karl Bühler (1990, p. 28), language serves simultaneously to *represent* (objectively), *express* (subjectively) and *appeal* (persuasively). Now these three functions are not equally represented in every linguistic expression. In a single text (or portion of text) the depictive element may be dominant, in another the expressive element, and in yet another the attempt to persuade hearers or readers. Of course the whole of a text will not always be dedicated exclusively to a single function. In actual practice there are constant combinations and overlapping. And yet as one or another of these functions becomes *dominant* in any given text, it becomes evident that distinguishing the three basic functions is justified: the depictive function is emphasized in *content-focused* texts, the expressive function emphasizing *form-focused* texts, and the persuasive function emphasizing *appeal-focused* texts.[28] By emphasis on content is meant a dominant interest in conveying certain matters, data or information. Texts emphasizing form will certainly have content, but it is the form employed for the content which is of dominant concern.

Up to this point our analysis has followed roughly the traditionally basic distinction between texts as pragmatic (emphasizing content) and literary (emphasizing form), although without accepting indiscriminately the traditional assignment of different kinds of text to these basic types, as the following will show.

Thus *advertising copy* should not be classified as content-focused, where it would be essential only that the informational content correspond to the original. Commercial advertising is a rather pointed example of the persuasive function of language, and in translating this must be recognized as taking priority over depictive functions. *Cheap novels*, on the other hand, belong to the "literary" type of texts despite their lack of literary quality. For purposes of translation and criticism it may appear foolish to identify them as

---

[28] This is a more appropriate name for the type which I earlier called *effect-oriented* (See K. Reiss, 1969) because the chief purpose of persuasion is to achieve a non-verbal effect. Unfortunately, however, the term *effect* too easily confused such practical results with the esthetic effects of a text.

form-focused texts, yet they enjoy a lively popularity because of
their exciting content, which is evidenced also in the quantity of
their translations. Since the readers have only a marginal interest (if
any) in esthetic qualities, the translator can hardly be expected to
devote time and effort to observing more formal aspects.[29]

Benedetto Croce (1953, p. 108 in Kloepfer, 1967, p. 57) indicates emphatically that in theoretical considerations of the problems
of translating there has been lacking any clear distinction between
the dimensions of logic and esthetics, of prose and poetry, and that
this has led to false theoretics. While the discussion of translation
has thoroughly confirmed the distinction between the logical and
esthetic dimensions of language,[30] in contrast a third dimension of
language has been ignored: dialogical. This has evidently been the
primary reason for ignoring the appeal-focused text type representing the persuasive function of language. Schematically the
corresponding relationships would appear as follows:

language function	representation	expression	persuasion
language dimension	logic	esthetics	dialogue
text type	content-focused (informative)	form-focused (expressive)	appeal-focused (operative)

As this schema shows, along with the two different text types
traditionally recognized a third, the appeal-focused type, must now
also be defined.

---

[29] See F. Ayala (1965, p. 29), "Si el autor mismo no ha practicado mayor
pulcritud estilística cuando escribía libremente, sin tener que ceñirse a un texto
ya dado y consolidado, ... ¿por qué había de imponerse el traductor semejante
carga?" ("If the author himself was careless about stylistic interests when he
was writing freely, feeling no necessity to produce a neatly finished piece, ...
why should the translator take any such pains?").

[30] See the explicitly attested distinction between pragmatic and artistic texts.

The appeal-focused type delivers a content, as do the other types, but in a distinctive linguistic form. Its structure is dictated by a particular perspective, reflecting a more or less clearly defined goal. Characteristically such texts aim at achieving a non-linguistic result, and their translation must preserve a clear appeal for action on the part of the hearer or reader.

In addition to these three text types based on the functions of language, however, there is a fourth group of texts which may be designated the "audiomedial" type.[31] Such texts are *written* to be *spoken* (or *sung*) and hence are not *read* by their audience but *heard,* often with the aid of some *extra-linguistic medium,* which itself plays a part in the mediation of the complex literary blend.

2.2.1 The content-focused text

Any practical attempt to organize the whole variety of materials for translation in a fourfold typology must begin by taking the major characteristics of each of the types and subdividing them into their varieties. While the *type* of a text concerns essentially the translation method and the relative priorities of what is to be preserved in the target language, the *kind* of text concerns the linguistic elements to be considered when translating.[32] Assuming this, the principal kinds of text in the content-focused type would include press releases and comments, news reports, commercial correspondence, inventories of merchandise, operating instructions, directions for use, patent specifications, treaties, official documents, educational works, non-fiction books of all sorts, essays, treatises, reports, theses, and specialized literature in the humanities, the natural sciences, and other technical fields.

---

[31] This is clearly better than calling it a subsidiary type as I did earlier (see K. Reiss, 1969). That term proved to be misleading because it implied for the text an auxiliary status which is actually provided by the associated extra-linguistic factors. The new name describes more accurately the specific character of the text type. [K. Reiss later changed the term to "multimedial" (Tr.)].
[32] See below 2.3 and 3.5.

However, a further point should also be clarified. If we draw a distinction between content-focused and form-focused texts, this is not to imply that content-focused texts do not have a form. Just as there can be no form of communication without some kind of content, there can be no kind of content that does not have some form. Consequently in dealing with content-focused texts it should also be remembered that since content and form are inextricably interrelated, *how* a thought is expressed is hardly less important than *what* is expressed. Only in the proper *form* is the *content* properly expressed.

To this extent we distance ourselves from the one-sided functionalist view of language, which sees it merely as the means of communication designed to accommodate particular units of information. Such a view of language is utterly inadequate for appeal-focused texts, because these are not concerned primarily with making a statement so much as with exploiting language as a tool in addressing a person, using language to provoke a non-linguistic response.

While a content-focused text is concerned with form as it relates to the effective communication and accuracy of information, a form-focused text is concerned with the esthetic and artistically creative nature of the form. Content-focused texts are judged in terms of their semantic, grammatical and stylistic characteristics, and this is reflected in their translation. Form-focused texts are judged in relation to their esthetics, as well as their stylistic, semantic and grammatical characteristics, and they are translated accordingly.

Reports, educational texts, inventories, etc., are obviously of the content-focused type. They are more or less anonymous, and generally designed to provide information rapidly, accurately, and comprehensively, or describe a situation. Commentaries are somewhat different. They are frequently written by distinguished commentators who have literary ambitions and distinctive styles. Although these texts may exhibit individualistic styles (which should be preserved in translation if possible[33] and also be considered among

---

[33] See further in the discussion of stylistic components, 3.4.

the criteria for evaluating the translation), they properly belong to the content-focused type because their *principle concern* is for the particular situation or event which they treat or comment on. Or, as Julius Wirl (1958) puts it:

> When we said above that an author's unconscious or half-conscious preference for a particular form of expression or style does not affect the essential character of a text, we had in mind an author whose full and undivided creative attention is focused on the content or material of an idea, and who considers forms of expression only for their relevance to a clear presentation of that content. Even when the author consciously selects a particular expression while focusing on fidelity to his experience and giving full consideration to alternative expressions, the relationship of form is always subordinate to that of content. The sole purpose of form is to give adequate expression to content.

If a topic and its discussion (i.e., its essential substance) are fully represented in a translation, the translation must be considered satisfactory.

It may be remarked that documents such as treaties and certificates generally observe a defined structure prescribed by official regulations. But it should also be noted that linguistic form must not be confused with technical formalities, which are concerned primarily with such superficial details as layout, prescribed formulae, etc.[34]

---

[34] In bilateral international treaties, for example, it is usual for the nation to be given precedence in the document written in its own language. An agreement between the German Federal Republic and Spain would read in the German text: "Abkommen zwischen der Bundesrepublik Deutschland und Spanien über gewisse Auswirkungen des Zweiten Weltkrieges. Die Bundesrepublik Deutschlands und Spanien ...;" but the Spanish text would read: "Convenio entre España y la República Federal de Alemania sobre ciertos efectos de la Segunda Guerra Mundial. España y la República Federal ..."

Formal regulations developed through traditional diplomatic usage also belong here.

These texts are related to texts in the humanities, the natural sciences and technical fields (treatises, essays and research reports, etc.), where the content can be satisfactorily translated only by using the special terminology and idioms of the respective fields.

Finally, in order to clarify the nature of non-fiction books (or non-fiction texts) as belonging to the content-focused type and yet distinguished from technical reference literature, non-fiction literature may be defined as general non-specialist treatments of the various fields. Of course, non-fiction writers may also have "literary ambitions."[35] The distinctive characteristics of non-fiction texts should be material accuracy, precise information and current language. There may, of course, be an occasional use of specialized technical terms, but in the end the critical distinction is the readership addressed by the author, which is determinative for choice of language. If the author has specialists in mind (textbooks or technical journals), the translation should observe a comparable precision in technical terminology. If the author is addressing a lay public of broader interests (non-fiction, general periodicals), the translation should show greater attention to stylistic matters.

The various kinds of text grouped together here as content-focused texts may be characterized as concerned primarily if not exclusively with communicating information.

Once a given text is identified as belonging to the content-focused type, an important component of its translation method has been determined. Content-focused texts require *invariance in transfer of their content*. The critic must above all ascertain whether their content and information is fully represented in the target language. This primary requirement demands that the linguistic form of the translation be adapted without reservation to the idiom of the target language; in other words, the form of the translation should be es-

---

[35] See R. Pörtner (1968, p. 32): "I believe ... that even a non-fiction volume is in no way harmed if its subject is approached with a sense of interest or excitement. By this I do not mean smuggling non-fiction into the sacred precincts of literature underhandedly or on the sly, but only that it should have a certain personal touch."

sentially oriented to the usage of the *target language.*

The second criterion for evaluating a content-focused text is the thoroughness of its orientation to the target language. The target language must dominate, because in this type of text the informational content is most important, and the reader of the translation needs to have it presented in a familiar (Jumpelt, 1961, p. 133)[36] linguistic form.[37]

2.2.2 The form-focused text

In order to describe more precisely this second type of text and the various kinds of text associated with it, we must first clarify the concept of *form* which is basic to it. In general, "form" is concerned with *how* an author expresses himself, as distinct from "content," which deals with *what* the author says. Of course this characterization is true for all texts, including pragmatic texts, as we noted in the previous section, and consequently it is too general to serve as a distinctive trait of form-focused texts. In these texts the author makes use of formal elements, whether consciously or

---

[36] R. Jumpelt uses the term "gebräuchlich" (*common*) and emphasizes the necessity of this for all technical texts. For notes on necessary transformations in rendering English or Romance language texts in correct but also idiomatic German translation with special reference to superlative forms, verbal periphrases and the passive voice, see M. Wandruszka (1969, p. 84, 338, 432).

[37] The target language is also of central concern in the appeal-focused type, because without full adaptation to the target language the effectiveness of an appeal cannot be assured. In contrast, the form-focused type is primarily controlled by the source language because the esthetic effect is based on formal elements which must be preserved. Of course this does not mean that the basic principles of the target language can be freely ignored (see exceptions in 6.6 and 6.7). The language of a translation, as J. Ortega y Gasset (1937, p. 88-89) puts it, should never be pushed to the limits of intelligibility ("al extremo de lo inteligible"), because in J. Grimm's (1963, p. 111) vivid metaphor, "trans*la*-*tion* is *trans*lation, traducere navem ("to lead a ship"): if one sets out on a sea voyage, plying with a ship fully manned and under full sail toward a foreign shore, he must eventually *put ashore* on *alien soil* where *alien winds* blow." (Author's emphasis)

unconsciously, for a specific esthetic effect. These formal elements do not simply exercise an influence over the subject matter, but go beyond this to contribute a special artistic expression[38] that is contextually distinctive and can be reproduced in a target language only by some analogous form of expression. Therefore, the expressive function of language, which is primary in form-focused texts, must find an *analogous form* in the translation to create a corresponding impression,[39] so that the translation can become a true equivalent.

Even a single sound can constitute an important formal element.[40] But even syntactical traits can be used as art forms.[41] The "tempo" of the style, as well as stylistic forms and rhyme schemes (von Wilamowitz-Moellendorff, 1963, pp. 148, 154), comparative and

---

[38] See J. Wirl (1958, p. 54): "Naturally, if the formal elements are not selected precisely because they are best adapted to express and represent a given content, and have themselves emerged in a process completely conditioned by the substance of the content ...." Similarly O. Kade, (1964, p. 277) "... because in literary translations the formal component functions not merely as a means of communicating the artistic structure, but also an esthetic value. Despite its strictly theoretical character, the formal component of a literary translation gives it a peculiarly individual quality."

[39] See S. von Radecki (1965, p. 46): "... I realized that the German translation had to produce the same impression as did the Russian text. The important thing was the impression: if a literal translation would not do it, recourse must be made to all the resources of imagination." See also H. J. Kann (1968, p. 127): "The number of colloquial expressions, on the whole, was perceptibly reduced in the German version [of Hemingway's *The Killers*]. But for the German reader, who does not expect colloquial expressions in a literary text, this modification preserved the intended impression."

[40] See R. Kloepfer (1967, p. 81): "A single sound has practically no significance in an artistic work except in relation to others; ... but when it stands in correlation to others (as in alliteration, assonance, rhyme or even euphony, in a phonetic or structural pattern) it becomes significant. In this sense an esthetic detail can become the most important element of the composition, not by itself but as part of a sequence."

[41] A. Luther (1949, p. 11) offers an instructive comment with regard to a translation of Tolstoy: "On comparing the translation with the original I find that the translator has recast Tolstoy's long periods into short crisp sentences. The broad and gently flowing river is converted into a foaming mountain stream. The content of the narrative is the same, but the form is completely altered."

figurative manners of speaking, proverbs and metaphors (Nida, 1964, p. 94) should all be observed. The meter and its esthetic effects should also be noted.[42] Phonostylistic elements are significant factors not only in poetry, but also in literary prose (Blixen, 1954, pp. 45-51).

How should a critic expect a translator to treat these formal factors? Obviously they cannot be taken over slavishly from the source language into the target language, and in any event for phonolinguistic elements this would be impossible because of the phonological differences between languages. In content-focused texts, where formal aspects are of secondary significance, they can simply be ignored, but not in literary texts where they constitute an essential factor. There the chief requirement is to achieve a similar esthetic effect. This can be done by creating equivalents through new forms.[43] Thus in a form-focused text the translator will not mimic slavishly (adopt) the forms of the source language, but rather appreciate the form of the source language and be inspired by it to discover an analogous form in the target language,[44] one which will elicit a similar response in the reader. For this reason we characterize form-focused texts as *source language* oriented texts.

---

[42] See among others E. Horst von Tscharner (1963, p. 274) and R. Kloepfer (1967, p. 99).

[43] "By new forms," M. Buber (1963, p. 353) insists, "is not meant a bold strategy of borrowing a term from a different context, but the attempt to create something corresponding within the linguistic structure of the foreign language in which the translation is made." Buber then goes on to say explicitly that only a translation inspired "by a similar motivation" can yield "a similar effect."

[44] A good example may be found in Aldous Huxley's, short story *Green Tunnels* (See H. J. Kann, 1968, p. 47), where the repetition of the same ending builds a sonority: "... feel*ing* about among superhuman conceptions, plann*ing* huge groups and friezes and monumental figures with blow*ing* draperies; plann*ing*, conceiv*ing*, but never quite achiev*ing*. Look, there's someth*ing* of Michelangelo." In the German translation by Herbert E. Herlitschka the ending *-en* assumes a similar function, although not in quite the same way: "... unter unmenschlich*en* Vorstellung*en* umhertast*en* und riesige Grupp*en*, Friese und Monumentalgestalt*en* mit flatternd*en* Gewändernentwerf*en*; entwerf*en*, sich ausdenk*en*, aber niemals ganz vollend*en*."

What kinds of text does this text type include? Generally speaking, all texts based on formal literary principles, and therefore all texts which *express* more than they *state*, where figures of speech and style serve to achieve an esthetic purpose – in a word: texts which may be called artistic literary works.[45]

The difficulties involved in assigning various kinds of text to the form-focused text type cannot be avoided by relying on their stated literary genres.[46] Even the labels provided by the authors themselves cannot be trusted. Since terminology is plagued by widespread ambiguities – not to mention the pretentious use of sophisticated labels – neither the translator nor the critic can safely avoid the responsibility of an independent analysis. For example, an essay in the spirit of Karl Muth, for whom the essential element of a true essay is its esthetic value, can be read for the sheer enjoyment of its form with little or no interest in its material content; the translator must necessarily translate it by the principles for form-focused texts, and the critic must evaluate it by the same principles. Sometimes a text is described by its author as an essay, as Ludwig Rohner (1966, p. 128) notes: "A strong and verifiable trend in recent German essays is actually a betrayal, degrading the essay to a treatise, from imaginative language to theorizing prose, from free experimental writing to a *simple statement* of conclusions, from friendly conversation to a prose monologue ...," so that whatever the label given it, the text should actually be translated as a treatise, a report, or some other variety of content-focused type, and the critic should evaluate it as such. The same is true of *belles lettres*.

In identifying a text's type the analysis must be independent of literary classifications. Thus, for example, all forms of pulp fiction belong to the content-focused text type, because the esthetic and formal dimensions are either lacking in them or trivialized (Foltin,

---

[45] See however the comments on "audiomedial texts" (2.2.4), which must be excluded here even if they may be classed as artistic works.

[46] As we have noted, the term "text genre" (Text*gattung*) preferred by O. Kade and R. Jumpelt for the various kinds of text and text types should be avoided as misleading.

1968, p. 242-270). They deal with information (content-focused), even if the information they offer is unreal or fictional.[47] On the other hand, light fiction belongs to the lowest level of form-focused texts. As Foltin (1968, p. 248) notes, it makes higher pretensions, partly because of its greater stylistic sophistication. Accordingly more sophisticated standards on the part of both the translator and the critic are called for and fully justified.

Nor can poetry be indiscriminately assigned to the form-focused text type simply as a literary art form. Lampoons as well as satirical poems must be assigned to the appeal-focused text type, because the primary purpose in the translation is to achieve the same non-linguistic effect in the target language.[48]

In summary, on the basis of the proposed principles we may say that form-focused texts include literary prose (essays, biographies, belles-lettres), imaginative prose (anecdotes, short stories, novellas, romances), and poetry in all its forms (from the didactic to balladry to the purely sentimental). While these forms all serve to convey some content, they lose their individual character if the original author's external or inner forms are not preserved in translation, whether in their poetic norms, their style, or their artistic structure. The necessity for precise identity of content, characteristic

---

[47] It is by no means pointless to be concerned with the problems of translating light fiction, despite the views of J. Ortega y Gasset (1937, p. 88-89) as well as W. Widmer (1959, p. 39 ff.) and F. Kemp (1947, p. 154). Not just "high" literature deserves to be translated. In contrast to Ortega's and Widmer's view, the varieties of light fiction are simply inadequately represented in native German literature. German writers seem not to have the talent of American and English writers for murder mysteries – a genre which both excites and relaxes, providing relief from everyday stresses. Good light fiction is far more readily found in French, English and American writers than among Germans, who are either too highbrow and pompous or too simple to produce crass commercial potboilers. But rampant mass consumption and thirst for foreign thrillers and cheap novels have brought translations of this kind of literature to the attention of critics. It is precisely because of mass consumption that translations which are at least linguistically acceptable could save readers from complete linguistic confusion.

[48] See further under *appeal-focused texts* (2.2.3).

of the content-focused type of text, becomes relatively secondary to the demands for *similarity of form* and for an equivalence of esthetic effect.

The critic must also determine whether or not the translator has taken "the step from the linguistic level to the literary level of operation" (as Georges Mounin [1967, p. 123] would say), giving the translation a "second qualitative component, the esthetic component of 'literary' polish."

A necessary result of the above requirement is that in contrast to the content-focused text type, where the language of the translation is dictated by the target language, the language of the form-focused type is dictated by the *source language*.

For example, in a content-focused text a play on words can safely be ignored in a translation without the invariance of content being impaired. In a form-focused text, however, it is necessary to find a comparable device to represent its literary and esthetic function.

If the different structures of the source and target languages make a similar play on words impossible, the alternatives are to use a different figure of speech that would have a similar esthetic effect, or to introduce elsewhere a wordplay native to the target language where the source language has none.[49]

In a content-focused text the information implicit in the source text must be fully and explicitly stated in accordance with the principles and usages of the target language. In form-focused text the linguistic form of the source text, and not just the information it contains, determine the form in the target language. When the original author uses an expression that deviates from *normal usage* – as practically every author does[50] – the translator of a form-focused

---

[49] See K. Reiss (1967, August) and F. Güttinger (1963, p. 75). Such a strategy is a legitimate means of preserving the esthetic integrity, and a principle valid for all varieties of form-focused texts. See also W. E. Süskind-G. von der Vring (1963, p. 14) and R. Kloepfer (1967, p. 117): "... usually the omission can be compensated by an equivalent in another position."

[50] See J. Ortega y Gasset (1937, p. 12): "Escribir bien consiste en hacer

text should also be creative in deviating from the norms of the target language, especially when such "erosions" have an esthetic purpose. When a critic notices such differences they should not be discounted as errors. And when the differences are not paralleled in the original it should first be asked whether they are transposed equivalents which are to be accepted as echoing similar esthetic effects elsewhere. The most thorough justification of this practice is the statement by W. E. Süskind (Süskind and von der Vring, 1963, p. 14): "The original author wrote with full command of his own language, and he can therefore demand exploitation of the full range of subtle implications peculiar to expressions which our language, and our language alone, can offer."

Thus the critic can judge whether the translator has succeeded in bringing the reader to the original text. He must lead him "out of his own world," but not unsympathetically unless, of course, it was the author's intention to be shocking (Mounin, 1967, p. 125). Yet it is precisely this popular artistic device that Ernst Merian-Genast's restrictive comment intended: "Just as the principle of accommodation can be overdone, so can the principle of alienation. If the translator's attempt to imitate the expressions of the original faithfully goes beyond the limits of normal usage, the result may become (as Schlegel put it) sheer gibberish" (Merian-Genast, 1958, p. 34).

In content-focused texts it may be completely legitimate to render idioms, proverbs and metaphors either by similar constructions or by figures of speech in the target language, due to the demand for conformity to the normal usage of the target language. But in form-focused texts it is appropriate to render idioms (and proverbs) literally – treating metaphors and especially the author's own metaphors the same way – and to resort to comparable common expressions in the target language only when this becomes uncomfortably strained or unintelligible.

---

continuamente pequeñas *erosiones* a la gramática, al uso establecido, a la norma vigente de la lengua" ("Good writing consists in constantly *teasing* the grammar, established usages, and dominant principles of language") (italics added).

For example, when the idiom "a tempest in a teapot" occurs in an English text, if it is a content-focused text a simple translation of the idea such as "zuviel Aufhebens" ("too much fuss"), or "unnötige Aufregung" ("needless confusion") would be adequate. But in a form-focused text an equivalent (and equally idiomatic) vernacular expression is demanded, such as "ein Sturm im Wasserglas" ("turbulence in a tumbler"). In an appeal-focused text, depending on the context, possibly an expression such as "künstliche Aufregung" ("all worked up over nothing") should be considered, because "künstlich" ("artificial", "pseudo-") has strong emotional overtones.

There is one further matter that translation critics should consider in this connection. Rendering a poetical text from a source language as a prose text in a target language cannot be called translating in the strict sense. If a work is composed according to the literary canons of a source language, a reproduction of it in the common vernacular prose of a target language is no translation. When no attempt is made to preserve any parallelism on the formal level, any kind of adaptation in the target language is conceivable, including free revision and paraphrase. Since such a process can have far-reaching implications (Kemp, 1965, p. 22f; Kloepfer, 1967, p. 22f; Nida, 1964, p. 157), the critic must give these factors due consideration in making any evaluation.[51]

2.2.3 The appeal-focused text

Appeal-focused texts constitute the third text type in our typology. Appeal-focused texts do not simply convey certain information in a linguistic form; they are distinctive in always presenting information with a particular perspective, an explicit purpose, involving a *non-linguistic* result. Triggering this result is the important aspect: a clear appeal to the hearer or reader of the text is essential in a translation. The linguistic form of any given informational content in an appeal-focused text is distinctly secondary to achieving the

---

[51] See further below in ch. 6 and 7.

non-linguistic purpose of its message. It should provoke a particular reaction on the part of the hearers or readers, inciting them to engage in specific actions. This brings to the fore the independent rhetorical function of language, which is theoretically present in every linguistic expression. A commercial advertisement can be simply an enticement without offering any information or intending to stimulate any esthetic impression.[52] This linguistic function of appeal must at the least be significantly present for a text to be assigned to the appeal-focused text type.

What kinds of text should be assigned to this type? The above definition suggests they would include all texts in which the element of appeal is dominant, with advertising, publicity, preaching, propaganda, polemic, demagogy or satire providing either the purpose or linguistic means of expression.

Both the form and the content of commercial advertising are at one in their overall goal of arousing consumer response. In the words of E. Carnicé de Gállez (1966, p. 52), "All commercial propaganda is actually based on the appellative function of language (Bühler), because it is concerned with leading the hearers both inwardly and outwardly toward purchasing the products recommended, moving them to action."[53]

Advertising is generally defined as "planning to influence a group of people to engage in a particular behavior" (*Großer Brockhaus*). As S. J. Hayakawa (1952, p. 344) notes, "It appeals to vanity, fear, snobbism and false pride." Here again the text will lose its specific character in translation if an analogous form in the target language will not produce a comparable effect.[54]

---

[52] In 1970 a radio advertisement had the punch line, "Only Persil is 100% Persil!" The informational element was minimal, but "100%" suggested a degree of absolute quality to appeal to a consumer demand for the best of the best.

[53] "En realidad, toda propaganda comercial se basa en la función apelativa del lenguaje (Bühler), porque trata de dirigir la conducta interna y externa del oyente para la adquisición de los productos recomendados, mueve a la acción."

[54] E. Carnicé de Gállez (1966, p. 52 f.) offers a brief discussion of linguistic resources used in advertisements and publicity materials which is relevant to other languages as well.

Missionary texts would include considerable portions of the Old and New Testaments[55] and other religious writings, the main purpose of which is to witness to a religious faith and convert others to it.[56] But secular texts designed to propagate and gain adherents for an ideology also belong here.[57]

Propaganda is promotional material for a particular world view or political purpose which frequently tends to become polemical, and in political hands it easily becomes demagoguery. Both polemics and demagoguery often resort to satire, as do all forms of negative propaganda.

Concepts such as propaganda and demagoguery are closely related to rhetorical texts. Yet it is just as true for appeal-focused texts as for the other text types discussed above, that they cannot simply be equated with categories of literary genres. The rhetorical text type includes not only content-focused and form-focused texts (lectures, memorials, eulogies and tributes) (Lausberg, 1998, p. 52, 55, 129, 130, 131), but also appeal-focused texts (campaigning, propaganda and rabble rousing).[58]

Polemic and satire can become the determining characteristic not only in speeches but in many other literary forms as well (news commentaries, tracts, debates, pamphlets, controversies, partisan

---

[55] Reference to the Bible as a whole (or sacred texts generally) is intentionally omitted here because it comprises such a variety of different text types. The Song of Solomon should be assigned to the form-focused text type, the Acts of the Apostles to the content-focused type. But the Letters of the apostles, which were primarily intended to establish the young churches in the faith, were largely missionary in character and should be regarded as appeal-focused texts.

[56] See E. A. Nida (1964, p. 46): "Religious communication has often had as a principal intent this *suggestive response*, accomplished by *verbal symbols relatively devoid of semantic content*." (Italics added).

[57] See P. Brang's (1963, p. 412) comment on translating the primary Marxist writings: "One of its purposes is to ... introduce Marxist ideas to non-Russian peoples, and to make them attractive in their languages – a task with certain similarities to the role of Bible translation in Christian evangelism – and in general to promote the mission."

[58] T. Pelster (1966) gives an extensive description of the linguistic and other resources employed to achieve desired effects.

writings, satirical poetry). For a text to be assigned to the appeal-focused type it should meet Ludwig Rohner's (1966, p. 324) qualifications for satire: "It is essentially *tendentious, involved in non-literary interests. Concentration on a particular purpose* inhibits the satirist's freedom and undermines the literary form."

These qualifying characteristics of satire defined by Rohner – tendentiousness, extra-literary involvement, and concentration on a particular purpose – are also the characteristics of all appeal-focused texts. They not only undermine literary form, as Rohner notes, but they also alert the translator to the importance of preserving these characteristics.

What translation methods are appropriate for texts of this type?

With appeal-focused texts it is essential that in the target language the same effect be achieved as the original in the source language. This means that the translator has to depart more from the content and the form of the original than in other types of text.[59] It goes without saying that any such changes from the original should not be regarded by the critic as violating the principle of fidelity. Content-focused texts require fidelity in reproducing every detail in the content of the original. Fidelity in form-focused texts requires a similarity in formal principles and the preservation of the esthetic effect of the original. Correspondingly in appeal-focused texts it is fidelity to the original means achieving the result intended by the author, *preserving the appeal inherent in the text.*

A few examples will demonstrate what this means in the actual practice of translation.

A commercial advertisement is intended to lead the hearer or reader to purchasing the product advertized. Not every language group, however, will have the same response to the same kind of

---

[59] See O. Blixen (1954, p. 58): "Pero es claro que el traductor no tiene absoluta necesidad de reproducir en este caso la misma figura ... lo único que debe tratar de conservar es el efecto satírico." ["But it is clear that the translator is under no necessity in this case to reproduce the same expressions ... but only what is needed to preserve the satirical effect"]. The principle stated here for satirical texts applies also to appeal-focused texts.

advertisement.[60] While in Germany orange juice may be advertised effectively with the slogan, "the concentrated energy of the southern sun," a literal translation of this slogan would hardly be as compelling in more southerly countries.[61] Such a translation would be meaningless for achieving the effect intended. Here an "assimilating translation" (Merian-Genast, 1958, p. 26) is absolutely necessary.

In Bible translating there are similar problems. Sometimes for purposes of establishing and strengthening the faith of believers, it is necessary for specific images to undergo a degree of adaptation to match the different characteristics of the target language and its culture. For example, when translating an account of a sea voyage in the language of the desert Indians of northern Mexico the *form* of the narrative was retained. But the missionaries found that a literal translation of the *content* – traveling over waves – could not convey the desired effect because in their remote desert world the Indians had no concept of waves, lakes or oceans. The solution was found by substituting the closest available concept: a swamp. This kind of radical adaptation to the different world of the target language and its culture is what E. A. Nida (1964, p. 160) refers to as "dynamic equivalence." The resort to such "dynamic equivalents" should be reserved to appeal-focused texts, and we believe that they should not be used as extensively as Nida suggests.[62]

Appeal-focused rhetorical texts frequently require quite drastic changes from the original. As Angel M. de Lera (1968, Feb. 29) points out, although in Spanish today the tendency of rhetoric is generally restrained and avoids bombast, yet in this it presents a marked contrast to German rhetoric. When translating Spanish speeches and public addresses into German there are many embel-

---

[60] See E. A. Nida (1964, p. 227) [for Bible translating]: "The extent to which adjustments should be made, depends very largely upon the audience for which the translation is designed."

[61] In Italy the same product is advertised by indicating the benefits of the potent vitamins it contains.

[62] See further at 4.5 and 6.4.

lishing details that have to be suppressed to avoid impressing the German reader adversely. What the Spanish reader may enjoy as oratorical flair will probably strike the German reader as excessively baroque, possibly distorting the total effect. The extremely demagogical addresses of Fidel Castro may provide a good example. A German on reading Castro's fulsome demagoguery in translation would more likely be turned off than would the illiterate masses in Latin America who are accustomed to an oral tradition abounding in repetition and relatively indifferent to Spanish rhetorical standards. Such speeches would never excite German readers or audiences without considerable adaptations – not of their content but of their form. In summary we would say that the critic of an appeal-focused text should observe first of all whether the translator demonstrates sufficient appreciation of the non-linguistic and non-literary purposes of the text, and whether the version in the target language conveys the same appeal or evokes the same result as the author expressed in the original text.

2.2.4 The audio-medial text

Audio-medial texts, as we noted above, do not represent the simple transcription of oral communications, but rather are more or less important components of a larger complex. They are distinctive in their dependence on non-linguistic (technical) media and on graphic, acoustic, and visual kinds of expression. It is only in combination with them that the whole complex literary form realizes its full potential.

What kinds of text belong to this type? Generally speaking, any text that requires the use of and a degree of accommodation to a non-linguistic medium in order to communicate with the hearer, whether in the source or in the target language. Primary examples would be radio and television scripts, such as radio newscasts and reports, topical surveys and dramatic productions. In these not only grammar and elocution[63] but also acoustics (as in

---

[63] "There is an amazing difference between a dialog read silently and a dialog

dramatic productions) and visual aids (in television and films) play a significant role. An appreciation and mastery of these factors makes all the difference between success and failure, whether in the original form or in a translation.

Also belonging here are all texts which combine words with music, from the most popular hits of the day to songs and hymns, to choral works and oratorios.

Audio-medial texts would also include all stage productions, from musicals to operettas and operas, comedies and tragedies. A basic distinction should be drawn, however, between translations of screen scripts, libretti and dramas for school or study editions on the one hand,[64] where interest is focused on the language, and translations intended for stage production on the other, where the actor's appearance and manners, the costumes, the scenery and acoustics, and for opera, operettas and musicals, the music all contribute to effectiveness.[65]

Audio-medial texts could basically also be classified under other types, such as the content-focused type (radio addresses, documentary films), the form-focused type (topical surveys, dramas), or the appeal-focused type (comedies, tragedies). But for the concerns of the translator and the translation critic, this would be inadequate.[66] It would be impractical to assimilate this fourth text type, where language is enhanced and complemented by other elements, among the three text types based on the functions of language.

---

as understood by a play's director or delivered by actors" according to Z. Gorjan (1965, p. 88).

[64] See further at 6.3.

[65] See S. Brenner-Rademacher (1965, p. 8): "While novels provide the reader with passages describing persons and their situations, supplying the actors' words with background, life and color, the theater goer is dependent on what the actors themselves say. Here the spoken word, assisted by the director, the stage setting, decorations and costumes, must provide the characterization, nuances, tone and atmosphere."

[66] See R. Kloepfer (1967, p. 86): "For the comedies of Plautus to be successful as modern theater, the translator's first commandment must be to make them playable (or in W. Schadewaldt's terms, they must be credibly 'speakable')." [Later on K. Reiss characterized this fourth text-type as "multimedial" variants of the three "basic text-types" Tr.].

A translation of a radio address should not only be faithful on the level of content, it should also conform to the spoken syntax of the target language. This is not equally imperative for a translation intended only for reading.[67] Languages differ far more in the rhythmic and intonational patterns of their spoken form than in their written forms. For example, a lengthy and elaborately constructed period in a Spanish radio presentation would be quite easily appreciated by a German *reader*; the oral form would be understood only by Spanish hearers accustomed to the rapid flow of the original language, while the German listening to an exact translation would be likely to lose the train of thought. Sometimes the simplification of syntax in a presentation is almost imperative.[68]

In texts where music combines to provide an integrating element, the spoken component cannot safely be considered independently. The principles of prosody differ significantly from one language to another, and the musical elements of an original work naturally conform to the prosodic principles of the source language. The text of an opera intended for production would sound odd, if not simply ludicrous, if the translator insisted on fidelity to its form or content in the target language at the expense of sensitivity to the melody, rhythm and flow of the accompanying musical score.

In dramatic productions, whether the written text is regarded as content-focused, form-focused or appeal-focused, George Mounin's principle holds true: "Fidelity to the words, the grammar, the syntax, and even to the style of the sentences in a text must yield to the priority of what made the play a success in its homeland. Effectiveness as a stage production is more important for the translation than

---

[67] This demonstrates what Jiři Levý (1968, p. 77) noted with regard to theatrical dialog: "Theatrical dialog is a spoken text designed for delivery to an audience. On the most elementary tonal level it follows that combinations of sounds that are difficult to pronounce or easily misunderstood are inappropriate."

[68] For a German example, see B. Berger, cited by L. Rohner (1966, p. 114): "A condensed, intricately balanced statement needs to be unpacked and made transparent. A complex sentence replete with qualifications can be fatal in obscuring the primary thrust of a statement. The radio essayist must develop a new way of speaking which, briefly put, avoids stylistic niceties and appreciates the value of the fleeting word."

concerns for particular poetic or literary qualities, and if a conflict
arises it is overall effectiveness that should determine priorities.
As Mérimée said, it is not the (written) text, but the (spoken or
sung) play that is to be translated" (Mounin, 1967, p. 137 [paren-
theses added]).

It is only to be expected that translating audio-medial texts would
raise such a variety of problems for translators. These complexities
go with the turf when dealing with texts influenced to a greater or
lesser degree by non-linguistic factors.[69]

In summary, it remains that a translation method appropriate for
audio-medial texts must preserve the same *effect on the hearer* that
the original has in the source language. Circumstances may require
even greater departures from the content and form of the original
than are required by appeal-focused texts.[70] In films the role of translation may become quite subsidiary, in extreme cases becoming
simply the model from which the final coordination is developed.[71]

All this must be kept in mind not only by the translator, but also
by the critic as fundamental to an evaluation. The translation of a
content-focused text demands fidelity on the level of content. A
form-focused text demands similarity of form and esthetic effect.
An appeal-focused text demands the achievement of an identical

---

[69] The special problems of language form and translation encountered in the
various kinds of texts subsumed here in the audio-medial type are the subject
of many and frequently valuable discussions, especially in F. Ayala (1965, p.
36); J. Buschkiel (1966, Mai 5, p. 13); P. F. Caillé (1965, p. 116-122); E.
Carnicé de Gállez (1966, p. 47-58); E. Hartung (1965, p. 10 f.); R. Kloepfer
(1967, p. 86-97); G. Mounin (1967, p. 135-147); R. Schottlaender (1966).

[70] See G. Mounin (1967, p. 145): "To all these questions ... the synchronization specialists respond that *anything goes* that makes the point ... And the
point is considered made if the audience reacts to the synchronized film in the
same way that the audience reacted to the original film, even if it involves
fresh inspiration." Mounin's statement here about film synchronization may
be expanded to apply to all forms of audio-medial texts.

[71] See R. Jumpelt (1961, p. 24): "... while in the setting of filming dialog the
critical factor may well be the necessity for finding expressions that effectively carry the meaning and match most closely the actors' lip movements."
See also the special issue "Cinéma et Traduction," *Babel*, vol. 6 (1960).

response. Correspondingly translations of audio-medial texts are judged by the extent to which they match the original in integrating the contributions of non-linguistic media and other components in a complex literary form.

2.3 The text type as a literary category of translation criticism

Ortega y Gasset was right in saying that "it is impossible, at least almost always, to express all the facets of the original text."[72] There is no question that preserving all the elements of the original in a translation is an impossibility.[73] So the evaluation of a translation should not focus on some particular aspect or section of it, as is so often done, but it should begin rather with a definition of its text type. Once this is done and the appropriate translation method has been identified, then the degree to which the translator has met the relevant criteria can be assessed. In other words, in a content-focused text, it is whether *primary* concern has been shown for accuracy of data; in a form-focused text, whether special attention *beyond* the general concern for accuracy of information has been paid so that rhetorical structures will achieve a comparable esthetic effect; in an appeal-focused text, whether it achieves the purpose intended by the original; in an audio-medial text, whether the relevant media have been accommodated and their contributions duly incorporated.

Every translation is a compromise and an accommodation to the larger context of life. But it is a compromise that has to be weighed very carefully. Schadewaldt (1964) calls this "the art of the proper sacrifice," which should be dictated for a text by its type.

---

[72] J. Ortega y Gasset (1937, p. 82): "Es impossible, por lo menos lo es casi siempre, acercarnos a todas las dimensiones del texto original."

[73] See E. Cary [1963, (chapter 7) p. 393]: "No created work can be preserved perfectly and without some slight differences. The necessity for translation includes the necessity of making a choice. Making this choice is part of the translator's responsibility."

Accordingly it is important to observe the order of priorities which differ for the various types of text. Georges Mounin (1967, p. 19) writes that "modern translations attempt to represent a foreign language word for word, construction for construction, and figure for figure whenever possible." The real problem in translating arises precisely when this becomes impossible. And as we have noted above, this problem can be solved only by conforming to the respective demands of the four text types. The translation of content-focused texts must give priority to accuracy of the information they convey, form-focused texts to the structure of their content, appeal-focused texts to the function of their appeal, and audio-medial texts to the conditioning factors of non-linguistic media.

Literature in the broadest sense of the term may be defined as compassing the total range of written expressions in a given language. Thus any text fixed in a written form qualifies as literature, and any text can be the basis for a translation. Therefore the first category for translation criticism must be the literary category, which deals with text types.

3. The linguistic components

Once the literary character of a translation has been decided, the critic may turn to a second category – the *language style*. This has to do with its *linguistic features* and their equivalents in the target language, namely, examining in detail how the translation process has represented the linguistic peculiarities of the source language in the target language.[74]

---

[74] This concept is not to be identified with lexical or syntactic units, but rather with individual "sense units". See O. Kade (1964, p. 276): "No linguistic unit (e.g., a word) can be held *a priori* to a single translation equivalent, whether as a general rule or even between any two specific languages."

Analysis into thought units is determined both by the structure of the language and the immediate context. The following example is taken from A. Malblanc (1961, p. 23 f.):

Translation is basically possible only because there are parallels between languages on the level of *langue* (language as a system). The act of translating involves choosing the optimal equivalent from among the potential equivalents on the level of *parole* (language as actually spoken) (Kade, 1964, p. 137).

Some examples will clarify the distinction between potential and optimal equivalents.

1. For the German word *Glas,* Spanish offers the following potential equivalents: *cristal* (*crystal*), *vaso* (*vase*), *copa* (*tumbler*), *vidrio* (*pane*). If the context has to do with windows, the best lexical equivalent would be *vidrio*. The French word *opération* would have as potential equivalents in German: *Rechnungsart* (*invoice*), *Operation* (*operation*), *Aktion* (*campaign*), *Eingriff* (*surgery*), *Geschäft* (*business*), etc. In a commercial context the nearest equivalent would be *Geschäft*.

2. For the Spanish word *compromiso* the potential equivalents in German would be: *Kompromiß* (*compromise*), *Verpflichtung* (*duty*), *Engagement* (*commitment*). In the sentence "En las negociaciones sobre este tema no llegaron a un compromiso viable" ("In the negotiations over this matter they did not come to a viable compromise") the nearest semantic equivalent in German is definitely *Kompromiß*.

3. "Ich erhebe mein Glas auf die Freundschaft zwischen unsern Völkern ...". ("I raise my glass to friendship between our nations ..."). Here it is the situation, celebrating a festive occasion with wine or champagne, that decides the proper equivalent of

---

Damit schritt er schnell den langen Flur hinauf und öffnete eine kleine Seitentür,
  1   2   3   4   2   5   6
die in einen Korridor führte.
  7   8   7
Ce disant, il remonta rapidement le long vestibule et ouvrit une petite porte de côté
  1   2   3   4   5   6
qui donnait dans un corridor.
    7   8

the lexical unit "Glas" as "copa": "Levanto la[75] copa y brindo
por ... ("raising a glass to toast ... = drinking a toast to ...").
And on the other hand the French expression "la troisième" can
have quite different meanings depending on the situation. In
musical circles it could refer to the third symphony of a com-
poser. In a military context it could designate the third company,
brigade, division, etc. For an historian it could mean the Third
Republic, and for a tourist it could be the third leg of a trip.
The absolute necessity for considering the context is obvious
from this example of a French elliptical construction (taken from
Haensch, 1967, p. 61).

4. "Hay un placer íntimo, profundo, en ir recorriendo un pueblo
desconocido entre las sombras" ("It is a deep and intimate pleas-
ure to go wandering among the shades of an unfamiliar town")
(Azorín, *La Ruta de Don Quijote*). Potential equivalents for the
"ir + gerund" construction in German include *langsam* (*slowly*),
allmählich (*gradually*), *nach und nach* (*little by little*), *in aller
Ruhe* (*calmly*) *etwas tun* (*doing something*) etc. The context,
however, suggests that the optimal equivalent here would be a
single lexical unit: in place of *langsam, in aller Ruhe gehen
durch* (*wandering through slowly, calmly*), the word *schlendern*
(*saunter*), for which there is no single Spanish equivalent.

For the English sentence, "Though he is poor, he is an honest
man," a completely parallel potential equivalent in German would
be "Obwohl er arm ist, ist er ein ehrlicher Mann." In a literary context rather than a colloquial dialogue the stylistically preferred
semantic equivalent would be "er ist zwar arm, aber ehrlich" (taken
from W. Friedrich, 1969, p. 127).

---

[75] The literal equivalent of "ich erhebe mein Glas" would be "levanto *mi* copa."
But to be actually equivalent the translation must consider the factor of usage.
In Spanish the possessive pronoun is used less frequently than in German.
"Levanto *mi* copa" would be unidiomatic, so that "levanto *la* copa" is re-
quired to avoid being woodenly literal and achieve a genuinely equivalent
expression.

Every act of translating involves first recognizing the potential equivalents, and then selecting from among them the one best adapted to the particular context, also considering how well each element in the translation unit fits the overall context. ·

On the one hand this decision depends on the linguistic context, as Harald Weinrich (1966, p. 23) has observed: "A wide range of associations can be suggested by a word in isolation, but not by a word in a text. The context determines the meaning. Words qualify each other and are mutually limiting, and the more so if the context is complete."[76] On the other hand, the *extra-linguistic* situation plays a critical role in determining the form in the target language.[77] Or in the words of Georges Mounin (1967, p. 61), "Translation is primarily and universally a linguistic operation," but yet "it is never solely and exclusively a linguistic operation."

Consequently, while on the one hand the semantic, lexical, grammatical and stylistic (i.e., the linguistic) components of a text must be recognized, on the other hand the influence exercised by non-linguistic factors[78] on the semantic, lexical, grammatical and stylistic fields must also be taken into account.

The interaction of both these factors (the linguistic components and the non-linguistic determinants) and the way they are dealt with by the translator provide critics with two further categories of translation criticism: linguistic and pragmatic. These two categories are

---

[76] M. Wandreuszka (1969) offers good examples of how strongly a word's meaning is affected by its context or its linguistic usage, e.g., p. 43, Spanish *el tiempo*, French *le temps*, German *Zeit* (*time*) and *Wetter* (*weather*); p. 48, French *parents*, German *Eltern* (*parents*) and *Verwandte* (*relatives*); p. 50, Spanish *huésped*, German *Gast* (*guest*) and *Gastgeber* (*host*); p. 112, 115, French *la matinée*, German *Vormittag* (*morning*) and *Nachmittagsvorstellung* (*afternoon program*).

[77] J. C. Catford (1965, p. 31) distinguishes between co-text (linguistic context) and con-text (situational context). We do not adopt this terminology here despite its conciseness because it too easily invites typographical confusion. And besides, at least in German literature on translation, "Kontext" is generally understood to refer to *linguistic* context.

[78] See further in section 4.

of the utmost importance for translation critics, because without them it is impossible to evaluate the quality of the equivalents chosen.

A good example is the following dialog from Juan García Hortelano (1962), and its translation into German:

> "¿Jugaste al tenis esta mañana? – Sí. ¿Qué hiciste tú con los niños en la playa? – *No sé*. Buscamos conchas, trepamos por las rocas, construimos un castillo."
> "Has du heute morgen Tennis gespielt? – Ja. Und was hast du mit den Kindern am Strand gemacht? – *Nichts Besonderes*. Wir haben Muscheln gesucht, sind auf den Felsen herumgeklettert ..." ("Did you play tennis this morning? – Yes. And what did you do with the children on the beach? – *Nothing special*. We hunted for shells, climbed on the rocks ...")

It would be foolish to point to the words "No sé" and argue that the translator didn't understand the words: Any grammar could show him that "sé" is a form of the verb "saber" meaning "to know;" consequently "No sé" means "I don't know," and translating it as "Nichts Besonderes" ("nothing special") is simply wrong. Actually the form of the word (1st person singular of the verb) should be enough to show that "no sé" cannot be taken literally, because people would normally know what they had done, and what was done is what the question was about. The setting provides the interpretative factor, revealing the contextual value of the expression to be a null-formula, properly translated as "Nichts Besonderes" ("nothing special"), or even better as "Ach, nichts" ("oh, nothing"), which is closer to the brevity of the source language.

A different scenario appears in the following example given by Günther Haensch (1968, p. 69): "Le délégué français *s'étonne* que le point n'est pas été inscrit à l'ordre du jour." The translation "Der französische Delegierte *wundert(e) sich*, daß dieser Punkt nicht auf die Tagesordnung gesetzt wurde" ("The French delegate *was surprised* that the item was not on the agenda") is linguistically impeccable (s'étonner = sich wundern = be surprised). And yet it deserves a critical comment. Considering the context of the statement von Haensch proposes the translation, "Der französische

Delegierte *äußert sein Befremden darüber*, daß ..." ("The French delegate *expressed his displeasure* that ..."). When his own motion is ignored in the agenda, a good delegate cannot simply be privately surprised – the "surprise" needs to be expressed. In this *situation*, where the speaker's character as a diplomat bears on his linguistic usage, the most appropriate and idiomatic translation is "sein Befremden äußern" ("to express displeasure").

3.1 The semantic elements

Considering (or ignoring) the semantic component of a text is a critical factor in preserving the content and meaning of the original text. Failure to recognize polysemous words and homonyms, the lack of congruence between source and target language terms, mis-interpretations and arbitrary additions or omissions are the greatest source of danger for the translator, and consequently offer the most inviting openings for the critic.

To determine *semantic equivalence* the linguistic context must be examined, because this is where it can be seen most clearly what the author intends by what is said. And in the words of Erwin Koschmieder (1955, p. 121), it is absolutely necessary to under-stand "what is *intended* by the expression in the statement being translated" if one is to translate it at all. In these circumstances the linguistic context involves the microcontext as well as the macro-context, neither of which has precisely definable borders. They vary by the linguistic and conceptual environment of what is being translated. And yet the microcontext usually embraces only the words in the immediate context, only rarely extending beyond the limits of a sentence, while the macrocontext can include not only the paragraph but the whole of the text. Both are critical for deter-mining the optimal equivalent on the linguistic level.

A few examples will clarify the influence of the microcontext and the macrocontext in determining linguistic forms.

1. "Al salir el sol me desperté." The potential equivalents for the Spanish "salir" in German are: *ausgehen* (*go out*), *abfahren*

(*depart*), *abreisen* (*leave*), *aufgehen* (*rise*, of stars), etc. The subject of the infinitive construction is "el sol" (the sun), which is a star. In this instance the microcontext indicates that the optimal *lexical* equivalent in German is "Als die Sonne *aufging*" ("when the sun rose"), or "bei Sonnen*aufgang*" ("at sunrise"). Thus for the translation unit "al salir el sol" there are two potential *grammatical* equivalents: a subordinate clause and an adverbial expression. Which of the two is optimal in this instance can be determined only by the macrocontext with reference to *stylistic* factors. The relevant considerations would be whether the lengthier subordinate clause or the briefer adverbial qualification fits better with the rhythm of the whole sentence, or again, whether the lighter vowel of "aufging" is preferable to the darker vowel of "-aufgang." Here the determining factor is not a linguistic component of the source language, but a stylistic perspective of the target language.

2. In the next example it is different: "Al salir el sol, me despertaba." In this instance the microcontext (the unit here is still the sentence) consists of two components on the grammatical level: (1) the imperfect tense of the perfective verb in the principal clause ("despertaba") indicates that a repetitive action is being described. This affects the form of the subordinate clause in the target language. The German translation cannot be "*Als* die Sonne aufing ..." (a single event; "*As* the sun was rising"), but rather "*Wenn* die Sonne aufging" (a repeated event; "*When* the sun rose"). (2) The choice between the two potential equivalents "wenn die Sonne aufging" ("When the sun rose") and "bei Sonnenaufgang" ("at dawn") is decided by the imperfect tense of "despertaba" in favor of "wenn" in the subordinate clause, because the component of repetition in the adverbial clause is not expressed in German without an additional lexical element such as "Ich erwachte *stets* bei Sonnenaufgang" ("I *always* woke up at dawn"). Again the decision depends on stylistic considerations which are determined by context in the target language.

3. Similar considerations are operative in the following example

from French: "Le remède pris, je me sentis mieux" (Alfred Malblanc, 1961, p. 195). German equivalents of *prendre* include (weg-, ab-, an-, mit sich) nehmen, fassen, ergreifen, etc. ("to seize, to take or carry away with one," etc.). The object "le remède" ("medicine") points to "nehmen" ("take") as the optimal equivalent. But the microcontext does not simply determine the lexical equivalent for *prendre*, it also bears on the grammatical equivalent of the absolute participial construction, which has no precise equivalent in German. The past tense (passé défini) of the verb in the principal clause rules out the possibility of contemporaneous action. The participle needs to be translated by an expression indicating a prior time. The translator may opt for an adverbial phrase, "Nach Einnahme der Medizin ..." ("After taking the medicine ..."), or for an adverbial clause "Nachdem ich die Medizin eingenommen hatte" ("After I had taken the medicine ..."), depending on stylistic considerations. The former would be best in a technical report, and the latter in a personal conversation.

4. An example from English may also be illustrative. "By refusing to take any food, he made him accept his proposals" (W. Friedrich, 1969, p. 85). The microcontext identifies the equivalent of "to refuse" as "verweigern." It also indicates that the subject of the gerundial clause is "he." There are two possible grammatical equivalents for the translation unit "by refusing to take any food": a prepositional phrase or a subordinate clause. Here again it is the stylistic considerations of the macrocontext that prove decisive, whether "Dadurch, daß er jegliche Nahrungsaufnahme verweigerte ..." or "Durch Verweigerung jeglicher Nahrungsaufnahme brachte er ihn zur Annahme seiner Vorschläge" should be preferred.

5. A couple of examples will demonstrate the importance of macrocontexts for determining a translation, and how they may extend, as noted above, from a paragraph to the whole of a work. To translate the title of an essay or a book appropriately, for instance, it may be necessary to read the whole of the text. The

title of Flaubert's "L'Education sentimentale" cannot be translated into German without knowing the whole work. The critic has to decide which of the following proposed solutions is preferable on the basis of the macrocontext: *Schule des Herzens* ("A School for the Heart;" H. Ruppert), *Erziehung des Herzens* ("The Heart's Training;" E. A. Reinhards, cf. "Sentimental Education"; Robert Baldick), *Schule der Empfindsamkeit* ("A School for Sentimentalism;" H. Kanders), or *Lehrjahre des Herzens* ("The Heart's Novitiate;" H. Widmer). Only the characteristic aura of the entire work can suggest whether the romanticist *Schule der Empfindsamkeit* or the low key *Lehrjahre des Herzens* offers the *optimal* equivalent.

6. And as a final example, in the small anthology *Alemania* by Julio Camba (1947, p. 20) the article entitled "Las ideas alemanas" ("German Ideas") begins with the words "Cuando Cándido llega al país de Eldorado, se encuentra a unos chicos que juegan en medio de la calle con brillantes y turquesas de tamaño descomunal" ("When Candido came to the country of Eldorado, he met some children in the street who were playing with enormous diamonds and turquoise gems"). Normal translation practice would suggest two potential equivalents for the name "Cándido": either the Spanish form of the name could be retained in the German text (if it were the name of a Spaniard, this would be preferred; Don Juan Tenorio would not become Herr Johannes Tenor), or the German form of the name "Candidus" could be used. In this instance, however, the macrocontext suggests a third potential equivalent. In the next paragraph (eleven lines below) there is the sentence, "Heine recuerda esta página de Voltaire a propósito de las ideas alemanas" ("Heine recalls this page in Voltaire with reference to German ideas"). This shows that when Camba mentions "Cándido" he has in mind the novel *Candide* by Voltaire. This completely rules out the possibility of retaining the Spanish form of the name in the German translation. The corresponding German form "Candidus" could be justified by the fact that the

Spanish author had converted the French name to a Spanish
form. But accepting the French form of the name "Candide"
would be the optimal solution, because educated German readers would be familiar at least with the title of Voltaire's novel.[79]

But since we are concerned specifically with the evaluation of
translation materials that are texts in a fixed written form, any judgment with regard to the effectiveness of the semantic component
should also make allowance for the fact that many "meanings" are
not represented explicitly in the text. Depending on the language
from which the translation is made, it can be critical for the interpretation in a dialog whether the translator grasps the proper
intonation for an expression. Thus "Llegas tarde" would be said
differently as the equivalent of the German "du kommst aber spät!"
("You are late!" said reprovingly), or "du kommst zu spät" ("You
are too late," as a simple statement).[80] Sometimes the emphasis simply marks the *main* point of a statement, and this can be represented
explicitly by a skillful arrangement of word order.

3.2 The lexical elements

If full equivalence with the source text is the criterion by which the
semantic components of the target text are to be judged, the standard for the *lexical* components must be *adequacy*. A kind of
mirror-image literal accuracy (word for word translation) so often

---

[79] See also F. Güttinger (1963, pp. 118 f., 120) and E. A. Nida (1964, p. 243).
What Nida calls the "lexico-grammatical features of the immediate unit"
corresponds with our term "microcontext;" what he calls "discourse context"
is our "macrocontext."

[80] In German the intonation can be implied by supplemental words; see Section 1 above. A good English-German example is given in F. Güttinger (1963,
p. 148): "Thou wilt not murder me?" the queen says to Hamlet. A. W. von
Schlegel translates, "Du willst mich *doch* nicht mordern?" because this is not
a question with an open answer. The expected answer is expressed in English
by the speaker's intonation, and in German translation it is implied by the
supplemental word.

demanded in the target language cannot serve as an objective criterion because the vocabularies of any two languages (with their structural and conceptual differences) simply cannot coincide completely.[81] Therefore the critic has to determine whether the components of the original text have been adequately carried over to the target language on the lexical level. This involves observing whether the translator has demonstrated competence in dealing with technical terminology and special idioms (Pelster, 1966, p. 63ff, esp. p. 78; Güttinger, 1963, p. 195ff), "false friends," homonyms, untranslatable words (Mounin, 1967, p. 62ff; Koschmieder, 1955) names[82] and metaphors, plays on words, idiomatic usages and proverbs,[83] etc. Naturally in any such investigation the respective requirements of the various types of text should also enter into consideration.[84]

For example, in a content-focused text a metaphor may be considered as translated quite adequately if it is represented in the target language by an expression of the same semantic value although not by a metaphor or a comparable image. A form-focused text, however, would demand that whether the metaphor be traditional or a new creation by the author, it should be represented in the target language by an equally idiomatic metaphor of similar value or significance,[85] whether a traditional one is available or a new one must

---

[81] See U. von Wilamowitz-Moellendorff (1963, p. 144): "... actually, we can almost never translate an individual word, because apart from technical terminology, two words in different languages never have precisely the same meaning."

[82] See here among others, F. Güttinger (1963, p. 76 ff).

[83] For the inclusion of these among lexical components, see E. A. Nida (1964, p. 95). For Spanish/German examples, see E. A. Seibel (1963, p. 11 f).

[84] This aspect is not sufficiently appreciated by O. Blixen (1954, p. 38 f.) in his discussion of translation problems with regard to idiomatic usages and proverbs. In contrast R. Kloepfer (1967, p. 93) offers some excellent observations, especially for the appeal-focused text – although he does not discuss them as such.

[85] For example (A. Malblanc, 1961, p. 330): "D'abord la surprise le *cloua* sur place" ("At first the surprise left him *riveted*") = "Dennoch blieb er vor

be created. This demand is not as difficult as it would seem to be at first sight. With reference to H. Weinrich, F. Vonessen and F. Schelling, Rolf Kloepfer (1967, p. 116) observes that "the bolder and freer the thought, the more specific a metaphor is, the easier it is to express it in another language. There is not just 'a common tradition of imagery that is shared by Western languages,' nor a range of concrete images shared by all humanity, but rather certain basic human 'structures of imagination' – whether paralinguistic or supralinguistic – by which the creative human spirit can conceive images of original insight." This applies also to criteria for appeal-focused and audio-medial texts. It is the same with idiomatic usages and proverbs.

The play on words represents another example of this problem. Word-play on the lexical level does not need to be imitated in texts that are content-focused unless they happen to find close parallels in both languages.[86] In a form-focused text it should be represented by some parallel structure, in the same passage if possible, especially if there is some reference to it later in the same text. Otherwise a similar play on words could be introduced in some other passage more conveniently adapted to the target language.

Überraschung wie *angewurzelt* stehen" ("He stood as one *rooted in position* by surprise"). Or, "Quel bon *vent* vous amène!" ("What good *wind* brings you here!") = "Welch guter Stern hat Sie denn hergeführt!" ("What lucky *star* has brought you here!"). Or (D. Murray, 1968, p. 54): "Bodidioms was now an *old hand* at writing political articles" = "B. war jetzt schon ein *alter Hase* ..." ("B. was now an *old hare* ..."); while in a content-focused text either "experienced" or "a veteran" would qualify as adequate. Similarly, "We are likely to *have our hands full*" = "Wir werden *alle Hände voll zu tun haben*" ("We will *have our hands full*") could be rendered in a content-focused text as "sehr viel zu tun" ("have plenty to do"). It is not the words of the metaphor, but the semantic value of the metaphor that should be translated (E. A. Nida, 1964, p. 94), and as with idiomatic expressions, it is their significance in their respective languages that must be considered. See also F. Güttinger (1963, p. 64).

[86] That is, unless the meaning of the entire passage depends on the word play. In that event there should be an explanation in a footnote (E. A. Nida, 1964, p. 195).

3.3 The grammatical elements

The evaluation of a translation with regard to the *grammatical* components of a source text must be governed by the criterion of
correctness, and this in two respects. Due to the fact that the differences between the grammatical systems of languages are frequently
quite great, it is the morphology and syntax of the target language
that clearly deserve priority unless there is some overriding factor
either in the nature of the text[87] or some special circumstance.[88]
Otherwise grammatical correctness is satisfied if the translation
conforms to usage of the target language and if the relevant semantic and stylistic aspects of the grammatical structure of the source
language have been understood and adequately rendered.

"Adequately" does not mean simply a similarity of expressions,
although in closely related languages among the Western cultures
this is frequently the case. Stylistic considerations or the status of a
grammatical element in popular usage may often permit a simple
substitution (the literal adoption of a grammatical form) in the target language as a potential equivalent, the *optimal* equivalent will
frequently require a transposition (a change of the formal grammatical and syntactical elements).

With regard to verbal aspects, Spanish, and also French and
English, have developed a rich variety of periphrastic forms that
illustrate both perspectives.

1. The stylistic factor

In translating the Spanish sentence "Solía madrugar" (soler + infinitive for frequent action) it would be quite correct in German to
say "Er pflegte sich sehr früh zu erheben" ("It was his custom to get

---

[87] For example, when translating a work in which grammatical standards are
ignored and the lines of tolerance are extremely permissive.
[88] For example, the purpose of the translation, as in an interlinear gloss for
students.

up early"), and equally correct to say "Er stand immer sehr früh auf" ("He always got up early"). The first equivalent would be the optimal equivalent in a formal style, but the second in a normal style.

It is the same with the sentence "Las rosas comenzaron a florecer" (comenzar a + infinitive for ingressive action). The equivalents in German would be "Die Rosen erblühten" ("The roses burgeoned;" formal style); "Die Rosen begannen zu blühen" ("The roses were starting to bloom;" normal style).

Similarly with "Elle ne cessait de poser des questions" (Wandruszka, 1969, p. 346). A correct German translation would be "Sie hörte nicht auf, Fragen zu stellen" ("She did not stop asking questions"). An equally correct translation would be "Sie fragte unaufhörlich" ("She asked incessantly"). The first solution reflects spoken usage, and the second a written style.

The English sentence "The German Empire has ceased to exist" (W. Friedrich, 1969, p. 57) can be rendered "Das Reich hat aufgehört zu bestehen" (a literal rendering), but also equally correctly "Das Reich besteht nicht mehr" ("The Empire is no more"). Doubtless the verbal periphrasis resounds like a proclamation, reflecting a higher style than the pedestrian adverbial phrase.

2. The idiomatic factor

Finally it is not a striking lack of common adverbs in Spanish that has led to the extraordinarily developed system of verbal periphrasis (Criado de Val, 1962, p. 103). Universally, that is, in most languages – as well as in Spanish basically – the adverb is used to define the action of a verb (Dietrich, 1955, p. 25). While Spanish tends to show a preference for periphrasis, the greater tendency of German is towards adverbs (Bausch, 1963, p. 208). From the perspective of language usage the optimal equivalent for the Spanish sentence "Continuó buscando el libro" would not be "Er *fuhr fort*, das Buch zu suchen" ("He *continued* to hunt for the book"), but "Er suchte *weiter* nach dem Buch" ("He *kept on* hunting for the book").

The same holds for Spanish periphrastic constructions representing incomplete actions. A potential equivalent of the Spanish

"Don Pascual se contenta con preguntarle por el camino" would be "Don Pascual *begnügt sich damit*, ihn nach dem Weg zu fragen" ("Don Pascual *is content* to ask him about the way"). But the more idiomatic and therefore optimal equivalent would be "Don Pascual fragt ihn *lediglich* nach dem Weg" ("Don Pascual asked him *only* about the way").

The factor of idiomatic usage becomes even more important for translation when no convenient and comparable expression is available to serve as a potential equivalent, and some form of structural adaptation is necessary to avoid an undue strain in the target language, as in the following German equivalents of English and French expressions: "Lach nicht *andauernd*" (literally "Don't laugh *continually*") for "Don't *keep* laughing;" "Er erschien *nicht*" ("he did *not* appear") for "He *failed* to appear;" "Du brauchst *unbedingt* Hilfe" ("You need help *unconditionally*") for "You *are certain to* need help" (examples from W. Friedrich, 1969, p. 57 f.); "Mein Bruder ist *eben* ausgegangen" ("My brother has *just* gone out") for "mon frère *vient de* sortir" ("my brother *has just* left;" literally "... *comes from* leaving"); "*Beinahe* wäre ich nicht zurückgekommen" ("I *nearly* didn't come back") for "j'*ai failli* ne pas revenir" (literally "I *missed* not returning"); "Du wirst es *bald genug* sehen" ("You will see it soon enough") for "tu *ne tarderas pas* à le découvrir" (literally "you *will not delay* to discover it") (Wandruszka, 1969, p. 336 f.).

Here again we must give due recognition to the demands of language usage, as we have noted before. Correspondingly when translating from German into French or Spanish not every passive construction has to be retained, because these languages also have a passive construction. As often as possible active constructions should be employed, because French and Spanish prefer active constructions.[89]

---

[89] See A. Malblanc (1961, p. 230), "En premier lieu l'allemand fait un emploi plus grand de la voix passive que le français, qui *préfère* la voix active." Also M. Criado de Val (1962, p. 102 f.), "... lo verdaderamente peculiar de la passiva

The examples we have considered demonstrate that it is important, if not absolutely essential, to be aware of the status and subtle overtones of grammatical components in the source language. As Lessing (1879, p. 11) remarked, "too meticulous a fidelity will make a translation awkwardly affected, because not everything that is natural in one language will be equally natural in another."

3.4 The stylistic elements

In the realm of *stylistics* the critic must decide whether the text in the target language exhibits complete *correspondence*.[90] Of primary interest here is whether the translation gives due consideration to the differences between colloquial and standard or formal usage observed in the original (as with the other linguistic components, always contingent on the type of text), and whether the differences between the language levels in the two languages are actually comparable.[91] It should be determined whether the translation takes into account the stylistic components of the source text with regard to standard, individual, and contemporary usage, and whether in particular stylistic aspects the author's creative expressions deviate from normal language usage. In standard German there is the stylistic principle of variety. If an author constantly repeats a particular expression in order to achieve a certain esthetic effect, the normal

---

alemana es la *frecuencia* de su uso, que contrasta con la *decadencia*, cada vez mayor de esta forma en las lenguas románicas, y sobre todas ellas en el español." (Italics added).

[90] In this connection we do not understand "style" in the narrow sense assumed by R. Kloepfer (1967, p. 85) when he states that "a translation is literary only if it has style", but in the modern and more comprehensive understanding of the concept implicit in Bally's work, that views style as referring to "a choice among the elements and forms available in a language."

[91] See E. A. Seibel (1963, p. 14): "Here we have to ask whether there is a clear-cut distinction in Spanish between the standard language and colloquial usage. The claim can probably be made that the distinction is fluid, and that there is no standard language which can be defined and contrasted with familiar, folk and regional usages as is the case, for example, in England."

principle of variety stands in contrast to the intention of this special style.[92]

These last criteria gain especial significance when judging the translation of form-focused and appeal-focused texts.[93] The mixture or inconsistency of styles in the original text should at least be represented in the translation of these two types of text, whether the author intentionally uses them (perhaps demagogically) for an effect,[94] or there is an actual error in the original text.

At this point we should discuss a translation problem which divides both translators and critics: whether an original text should be "improved." In deciding this question it is again relevant to consider the type of text. In a content-focused text it is always appropriate to eliminate obvious errors and compensate for stylistic

---

[92] See C. Hoeppener (1953, p. 53 ff.): "In the first chapter of *Little Dorrit* Dickens depicts a summer day in Marseilles, a picture of a city burning under a blazing sun, staring at the fervid sky and stared at in return, with its staring white walls, its staring white streets, etc. This universal 'staring' which made the eyes ache is repeated so often on the page – some twenty times – that it arouses in the reader the same intolerable aching that the residents of Marseilles felt on this burning day in the staring white city .... The translator cannot reduce the twenty times to just two without violating the author's style, his distinctive use of language."

[93] See O. Blixen (1954, p. 20 f.): "En cambio los problemas estilísticos se darán normalmente en la traducción literaria, y puede afirmarse como regla que su importancia estará en razón directa de la peculiaridad del lenguaje del creador, o sea de su grado de apartamiento de la norma de la lengua en que escribe, y, además del realce que en la obra original tenga la forma externa, es decir, la expresión, frente al contenido." ("On the other hand, stylistic problems are generally found in literary translations, and it can be stated as a rule that their importance will be directly related to the degree that the author's language is distinctive, or the extent to which it departs from the standard usage of the language, and further, the relationship in the original work of the external forms, i.e., the expressions, to the content.")

[94] See T. Pelster (1966, p. 90): "Frequently a speaker will use an unexpected (or inconsistent) expression intentionally to arouse the hearer's attention. In such instances there is no question of defective usage" – whether in the original or in its translation. On the contrary, the translator who "corrects" the inconsistency because it is found offensive is at fault for ignoring the needs of the appeal-focused text.

defects.[95] In a form-focused text, on the other hand, a translator's stylistic or other faults should not be ignored "in a spirit of brotherly love" as Güttinger (1963, p. 107) advises, although elsewhere he warns that "the translator must be able to resist the temptation to clarify and improve the original." In a similar sense Walter Widmer (1959, p. 82) supports the view that the translator is obligated to represent the original clearly. Yet this view contrasts with the principle enunciated by Wilhelm von Humboldt (1963, p. 84) that "... where the original suggests without openly stating, where it uses a metaphor whose relevance may not be obvious, or where it omits a transitional point that is necessary for the reader, it would be unfair of the translator to supply arbitrarily a degree of clarity that is lacking in the text." This principle should hold for all aspects of all form-focused texts. Probably with A. Fraser Tytler in mind, A. W. von Schlegel (1846, p. 228) claims that "even unfortunate stylistic characteristics" should be preserved "in translations of poetry."

In any event, translators will most probably acknowledge the principle that critics should regard it as a self-evident presupposition never to make a judgment without first consulting the original. It has long been a common practice among some who claim to be translation critics to examine only the translated version, and to blame the translator instead of the author when the translator has faithfully reproduced all the flaws in the original.

3.5 Linguistic elements as a linguistic category for translation criticism

Only a true understanding and interpretation of the semantic, lexical, grammatical and stylistic elements of a text can preserve the meaning of the original in a target language. And it is precisely here that the principal problem of translation between natural

---

[95] See R. Jumpelt (1961, p. 39): "In contrast to translations of *belles-lettres*, which should be more or less impeccable, it is a specific condition of translations in the natural sciences that formal defects must be rectified" (and Jumpelt observes that in this type of text they are exceedingly frequent).

languages is defined (Oettinger, 1963, p. 436). The critic must examine the translation with regard to each of these linguistic elements, the semantic elements for equivalence, the lexical elements for adequacy, the grammatical elements for correctness, and the stylistic elements for correspondence. Attention must be paid to how each of these elements relate not only to each other, but also to the demands of their text type. On the one hand these elements are not independent entities;[96] on the other hand their value differs in each of the various text types. In content-focused texts verbal semantics (the lexical element) and syntactical semantics (the grammatical element) assume priority, while in form- and appeal-focused texts the phonetic, syntactic and lexical elements are especially important.

Just as the type of a text is a reliable guide in selecting an adequate translation method, so the kind of text generally determines the order in which the linguistic elements should be considered. For content-focused texts, for example, this would mean that the semantic element would take priority in all the different kinds of text. In a report this would be followed by the grammatical element, but in a technical work the lexical element would be a close second, while in a work of popular science the semantic and stylistic (individual style) elements would take precedence over lexical and grammatical elements for finding equivalents in the target language. Other text types would show similar patterns of sequence.

4. Extra-linguistic determinants

The critic must not forget that judgments about equivalents chosen in the translated text for the linguistic elements of the source text will inevitably be unsatisfactory if the extra-linguistic determinants which radically affect both the form of the original and also the version in the target language are not considered. It is precisely these

---

[96] There is, for example, a semantics of words, of syntax, and of style, just as "the stylistic system of a language may find expression in phonetic as well and grammatical and lexical semantic forms" (Kade, 1964, p. 145), an observation repeatedly demonstrated in the examples given above.

which frequently make all the difference whether an equivalent is optimal or simply potential. But what is meant by extra-linguistic determinants?

These include a broad range of extra-linguistic factors enabling the author to make specific choices among the variety of means available in his mother language which would not only be intelligible to the reader or hearer, but under certain circumstances would even permit him to ignore certain linguistic means and still be understood by members of his language group. Since all of these factors have an influence on the linguistic form of the text, they are designated extra-linguistic *determinants*.

For example, a Spanish author's alternatives to indicate a causal relationship such as a subordinate clause, an infinitive construction or an adverbial expression, remain a matter of (linguistic) style. The linguistic (i.e., grammatical and stylistic) elements suggest to the translator how to find optimal equivalents. Whether the Spanish author will choose the word "copa" or "vaso" in a particular instance depends on the situation, i.e., on an extra-linguistic factor: in proposing a toast the choice will be "copa" (a wine glass), but asking for water would make it "vaso" (a simple drinking glass). The matter of time can make a similar difference in the choice of words, as in the expression for the representative in the Spanish parliament. With reference to the period of the Second Republic (1931-1936) the word would be "diputado," but after the civil war (after 1939) the term would be "procurador (en Cortes)." Güttinger (1963, p. 118 ff.) cites an even more complicated example: whether the English word "dinner" should be translated as a noon meal, an evening meal or something else depends completely on the matter of time. The word originally referred to the noon meal and today it is usually the evening meal, but in the first half of the 18th century the main meal was properly served in the afternoon (about 4 or 5 o'clock).

The extra-linguistic determinants have to do with extra-linguistic conditions that affect linguistic forms. As Harald Weinrich (1966, p. 19) stated elsewhere, "Words belong to sentences, texts, and situations." Applying this thesis in our terminology, "sentences" are the microcontext, "texts" are the macrocontext and "situations" are the extra-linguistic factors which in this sense constitute the *situational* context. These terms summarize what F. A. Nida (1964, p. 243) calls on the one hand the "communicative context" (= circumstances involved in the original communication, including such matters as time, place, author, audience, intent), and on the other hand the "cultural context of the source language."

Georges Mounin (1967, p. 120) was concerned with the problem of extra-linguistic determinants (without using the term), although only in connection with "literary translations." He wrote: "... while it reserves to the concept of context all the information *explicitly* derived from the written literary text, for linguistic science the *situation* comprises all the geographical, historical and cultural data that are *not always* verbally expressed, and yet are necessary for a full translation of the meaning of the expression" (italics added). He then draws the following conclusion: "Translation today does not mean simply observing the structural and linguistic meaning of the text, its lexical and syntactic content, but rather the whole meaning of the statement, including its environment, century, culture, and if necessary the whole civilization which produced it" (p. 121).

In view of their complexity, any attempt to lay out the linguistic factors in the "situation" for purposes of translation and translation criticism in such categories as geographical, historical, social and cultural aspects seems altogether too vague. Consequently we should attempt to modify the present understanding of situational contexts as represented by Nida and Mounin, and develop it further. To this end in the following pages we will consider extra-linguistic determinants significant for translators and translation critics as they are related to situations in the narrow sense, to the facts concerned, their time and place, to the hearers, to the speakers and to the subjective implications involved.

4.1 The immediate situation

As already mentioned, all extra-linguistic determinants may be broadly characterized as contextual factors. But this is quite distinct from the significance of special situational determinants in an immediate context. As stated above, extra-linguistic factors may on occasion permit an author to reduce to a minimum the linguistic form of the message to be conveyed, because the hearer or reader will be able to supply the rest of the situation in his own language. This has to do with the immediate context, and not an entire work (in the technical linguistic sense of the term *situation* [Mounin, 1967, p. 120]), but for single passages and moments. Examples would be interjections, allusions (to literary works, historical events, fashions and the like), shortened colloquial expressions (e.g., "du kannst mir...!" ["You may ..."]), etc. Such expressions are found very frequently in the volatile dialogues of plays and novels. Such texts leave translators quite helpless unless they are able to imagine themselves "in the situation" of the speakers. Only then can they be in a position to find an optimal equivalent in the target language that will enable the reader of the translation to understand both the words and their context. Critics must also similarly place themselves "in the situation" to be able to judge whether the translator has chosen the proper words not only lexically but semantically as well. Quite often the microcontext and the macrocontext alone are not enough.

A conversational scene from *El Jarama* by Raphael Sánchez Ferlosio (1956, p. 38) offers a good example of this. The text teems with overtones and allusions. A literal translation would be awkward, to say the least, if not altogether incomprehensible. The translator has to take into consideration not just that the conversation here is between youth about twenty years old (the speaker factor) from the environment of the middle class bourgeoisie of Madrid (the place factor), and that their language reflects normal everyday usage without any special kind of jargon (lexical and stylistic elements). Instead, in order to understand the semantic value of many shortened or interrupted expressions, the translator must imagine as accurately as possible the scenes being described, putting himself into the character and the position of each of the persons in order to find equivalents for the interplay of half-expressed suggestions that vividly reflect the vitality of the actual scene: a hot summer day, anticipation of a refreshing dip in the river, and also a growing irritation on the part of one of the group who has imbibed a little too freely.

In summary we can say that the immediate context influences the lexical, grammatical and stylistic aspects of the form taken in the target language, and as such helps to interpret appropriately the semantic elements implicit in the original text.

4.2 The subject matter

An influential factor affecting the linguistic form of not only the original but also of its translation is the subject matter. Every text requires that the translator be sufficiently familiar with its field to be able to construct a lexically adequate version in the target language. *Rem tene*, as Cato said, and *verba sequentur* ["Know your subject, and the words follow"]. This is obviously true for all purely technical texts, where the terms and idioms have to accord with the common usage of the target language. But concern for subject-related factors is not at all peculiar to texts dealing with a specialization, but is common to all texts where translation requires an intimate knowledge of the subject. "The technical knowledge a translator needs for translating a novel about surgeons, aviators and high finance," F. Güttinger (1963, p. 103) suggests, "can be acquired as necessary. But far more importantly, the translator is expected to have the encyclopedic knowledge of a reference librarian." In a nutshell, whether translating a text or evaluating the translation, it is not enough to know the words – it is necessary to know what the words are about (Mounin, 1967, p. 107). Peter Brang (1963, p. 419) cites a perfect example: "The Russian translator of *Maria Stuart*, who was familiar with the words 'Rose' ('rose') and 'Kranz' ('wreath', 'garland') but not with 'Rosenkranz' ('rosary'), interpreted Schiller's stage direction as referring to a 'rose garland' – which led the producers in many theaters to make their heroine wear one in a sash or belt."

In summary, it all goes to show that the subject matter of a text must be understood and duly recognized by the translator and by the critic as well. Still the subject-related determinants are in the broadest sense primarily on the lexical level in the target language. Further, a translation of a technical text may have a strong component of foreign loan words, otherwise it may run the risk of appearing unprofessional.

4.3 The time factor

The time factor usually becomes relevant if the language of a text is intimately associated with a particular period. It naturally has an effect on translation decisions. In translating old texts the selection of words, antiquated morphological or syntactical forms, the choice of particular figures of speech, etc., should accord as closely as possible to the usages of the source text. All the more so as language is a living, ever changing organism, molded by specific circumstances which should be reflected in the translation – especially in form- and appeal-focused texts. The translation of an 18th-century text should essentially be distinguishable from the translation of a 20th-century text, even if the translator is of the 20th-century. This cannot be done by relying exclusively on the particular elements characteristic of the source text, because in contemporary usage these could seem to lead sometimes to quite different optimal equivalents. W. Widmer (1959, p. 60) quite rightly criticizes a translation of Balzac's novel *La Cousine Bette* for ignoring the time factor by saying that "besides, it is so saucy, pert and racy that it could be turn-of-the-century Berlin instead of Paris in the 1830s."

The time factor is also important in another sense for translation criticism. Thus the translation of a 19th-century text made about the same time cannot be judged by the same standards as a more recent translation of the same text, because the language of the original may not have changed, but the target language has been developing in the meanwhile. These factors may be particularly significant for form-focused and appeal-focused texts.[97] The familiar

---

[97] A good example of this is in R. Kloepfer (1967, p. 94 f). A comedy by

phenomenon of aging translations is operative here. This is the reason why the old classics of world literature need to be translated anew from time to time.[98] Julius Wirl (1958, p. 74) points out another effect of the time factor: "Advances in historical, philological and text critical research can (basically) alter traditionally accepted understandings of a literary or poetical work as well as affect the overall import and specific details of a text." An excellent example is provided by the many translations of Dante, especially the most successful versions, which not only reflect the language of the original but represent the respective stages of their target languages when they were translated, and not least demonstrate various concepts of the function of a translation.[99]

Plautus achieves comic effects by making use of suggestions from everyday life, such as fashion trends. Kloepfer produced an imaginative and effectively equivalent translation of a characteristic portion of this comedy showing "at the same time how short-lived a timely translation of a comedy need be if like the original it is aimed to satisfy a brief and specific moment" (p. 96). This translation which was designed ideally for 1965 with the catchwords of the period, would have to be altered considerably today.

[98] See E. Tabernig de Pucciarelli (1964, p. 139): "De esto depende que mientras las obras originales pertenecen a todos los tiempos y son definitivas, las traducciones son provisorias. En su mayoría son productos históricos y como tales envejecen y necesitan ser renovadas de acuerdo a nuevas exigencias de la sensibilidad, a nuevos intereses intelectuales o estéticos, a una nueva comprensión del original." ("This is the reason that while the original works are ageless and definitive, their translations are provisional. Most of them are historical products, and as such they grow old and need to be renewed to meet the needs of new sensibilities, new intellectual or esthetic interests, and new understandings of the original").

[99] See O. Blixen (1954, p. 43): "Pero con la traducción sucede otra cosa: ella envejece *siempre*, pues al plasmarse en la lengua de un determinado momento histórico vase cargando paulatinamente en algunos siglos – no necesariamente muchos – con el peso de toda la tradición idiomática y literaria de esa lengua" ("But with translation something else happens: it *inevitably* ages, since it is formed at a particular historical moment in the language, little by little through the years – sometimes more rapidly – it settles under the weight of the whole literary and idiomatic tradition of the language"). Yet we cannot share Blixen's view that original works do not age but only fail to match the *taste* of a new era. Blixen's misunderstanding here is probably due to his preoccupation with examples in Latin. Now Latin is a dead language and not continuing to de-

In this connection one more viewpoint should be noticed, although as a category for translation criticism it should be mentioned later. A translation may have a special purpose which may justify the time factor being legitimately ignored. The adaptation of Middle High German texts in contemporary German may be justified if their purpose is to make them intelligible to the modern reader. Similarly Old French texts may be translated into contemporary German as an aid to their understanding by the modern reader.

From what has been said it may be inferred that the time factor is a very complex determinant, and that its consideration demands very sophisticated sensitivities, both linguistically and stylistically, depending on the type of text and also the special interests of the translator and the translation critic.

One example will show how the most appropriate word and the standards for its critical evaluation can vary within a brief time span. In a critique (Mager, 1968) of the novel *La familia de Pascual Duarte* by Camilo José Cela (1945) the writer listed under the rubric "Changes from the original" the following passages: "No obstante, y si *la Providencia* dispone que ..." ("Nevertheless, if Providence should permit;" *Pascual Duarte*, p. 22) and the translation "Wenn es aber *das Schicksal* will, daß ..." ("But if fate should decree;" *Mager* [1968], p. 15 ff.). His complaint with the translation of *la Providencia* by *Schicksal* was: "With due respect to 'free' translation, it does not give the translator the right to take a religious concept, which came naturally to the Spaniard (whether consciously or unconsciously) from his deep background in the faith, and convert it to an "Enlightenment" idiom. Although it would make the

---

velop. Living languages are developing languages, and consequently all linguistic products age and are dated, *whether they are originals or translations.* Translations may age more rapidly, especially if the target language is changing more rapidly and noticeably than the original language. This brings in the factor of phases, which equally with the time factor can affect translations. The Spanish of the 16th century was already fully developed. German translations from the Spanish are hardly readable today because German has developed far more extensively since the 16th century than has Spanish.

translation read like an original in German, the reader should be aware that he was dealing with Spaniards." (p. 49-50). The criticism is essentially right. Instead of *Schicksal* the word *Himmel* ("heaven") would have been better, but not *die Vorsehung* ("Providence"), as the author suggested in conversation. In 1949, the year the translation appeared, the word *Vorsehung* had such a fatal ring to it through Hitler's demagogical abuse of the term that a German translator would have avoided it if at all possible. It would inevitably have evoked for the German reader in 1949 associations that had nothing to do with the original and would have amounted to mistranslation. The translation critic evidently never thought of this time factor as relevant for the text in the target language.[100]

The above examples make it quite clear that the translation critic should always consider very carefully what alternatives the translator could have weighed beyond the obvious ones. This could also well contribute to turning a negative criticism into an objective judgment.

4.4 The place factor

The place factor can present the translator with even greater difficulties as a determinant than the time factor. Place factors include primarily all the facts and characteristics of the country and culture of the source language, and further also any associations of the scene where the actions described take place. It is especially difficult to translate into a target language lacking similar kinds of places, attempting to describe things which are beyond the range of its speakers' imagination. Although the problem this poses for translation should not be minimized, yet it can be argued against Ortega y Gasset (1937, p. 20f) that difficulties of this kind do not make translation a utopian exercise, especially when the two languages share

---

[100] Another good example is in G. Mounin (1967, p. 141): Merimée rewrote an entire passage in his translation of a piece by Gogol in order to avoid using the word "démolition," because the demolitions undertaken in Paris in his day gave it a bad ring.

a common culture (Reiss, 1968, p. 377f, note 13). And further, these difficulties are lessened day by day thanks to modern mass media and the growth of tourism which have greatly increased everyone's awareness of environmental diversity. Ortega gives the example of the Spanish word *bosque* ("forest") and the German word *Wald* ("woods"), pointing out how great a difference there is between the realities represented by these two words, their atmosphere and the instinctive associations they arouse, and correspondingly the concepts they represent to Spaniards and Germans respectively. Undoubtedly these terms lack a common consistency of image, emotional aura and associations. But a competent translator familiar with the country can approximate the meaning far more closely by concentrating on the attributes of places, i.e., by not translating the words, but the realities they represent. In view of this, the translation critic must be able to understand the motives of the translator if he is to give due weight to the influence of place factors. Of course it is to the advantage of both the translator and the critic to be personally familiar with the places discussed. The translator could deal with the present instance of the Spanish word *bosque* by translating it, depending on the context and style of the passage, as *Wald*, *Wäldchen* ("copse"), *Hain* ("grove"), *Gehölz* ("spinney"), etc., or in reverse, the German *Wald* could be rendered as *monte* ("woodland"), *soto* ("grove"), etc. Yet finally what may be taken as a communicational defect[101] is not really a translation problem but rather a universal human problem which affects communication between speakers of the same language. For a person who has never been outside the Ruhr valley the word *Wald* will not have the same meaning that it has for one from the Black Forest, and it is altogether improbable that the word has for today's youth

---

[101] See E. Cary (1963, p. 393): "Certainly the act of communication ... is never perfect. Much is lost in the process, and this is as true for the printed page of translation as for the foreign country that is being described or the distant past which is being revived. It is impossible for the end result to be perfectly identical without a difference." On the concept of communication, see G. Mounin (1967, p. 92 ff).

the same emotional overtones as it had for poets of the Romantic period.

Handling problems related to the place factor becomes especially demanding for translators when discussing circumstances and institutions, customs and habits that are peculiar to the country of the source language.[102] Robert L. Politzer (1966, p. 33f) calls these "culture-bound translation problems" and believes that "the typical culture-bound problem arises simply from the fact that the situation or institution, or even the abstract idea in a particular culture is alien to another culture (and therefore to its language). But when Politzer adds the opinion that this translation problem is basically insoluble, he challenges the experience of every translator.[103] Genuine possibilities for overcoming these difficulties include: 1. loan words, i.e., "borrowing not only the concept but even the source language's word for a cultural socio-economic institution or event peculiar to the source culture" (Kade, 1964, p. 105) (recent examples include junta, guerrilla, teenager, kolkhoz); 2. calques or loan formations, constructing new words in the target language (e.g., Wolkenkratzer for skyscraper, Nietenhose for studded jeans, Schnellbrüter for fast breeder [reactor]); 3. using the foreign expression and adding an explanatory footnote; 4. an explanatory translation (e.g., cocido – a stew, Retiro – a park, Sacré-Coeur – a church, Puzzle – a game, etc.).[104]

These four possibilities should not be used indifferently, but

---

[102] See O. Kade (1964, p. 99): "These phenomena are frequently designated 'realia' (realities). They include such socio-economic and cultural events and institutions (in the broadest sense) as are peculiar to the socio-economic structure of a given culture."

[103] See O. Kade (1964, p. 99): "... so there is no basis for the assumption – which is also refuted by experience – that realia [realities distinctive to a culture] may give rise to at least temporarily insoluble, translation problems."

[104] These methods of providing identifiers to clarify a translation correspond largely to the suggestion of E. A. Nida and C. Taber (1969, pp. 109, 198) of supplying *markers*, "when certain completely unknown terms are borrowed." Examples would be "*precious stone* ruby, *city* Jerusalem, *rite* of baptism, a linen *cloth*, the *sect* of the Pharisees, etc."

employed judiciously according to the demands of the particular text type at hand as well as the kind of text involved. Many kinds of content-focused texts welcome the possibility of footnotes (translations of scholarly and non-fiction works). On occasion a description of the situation which is alien to the target language may be introduced into the text itself. Appeal-focused texts, which generally avoid footnotes, and also purely technical texts prefer the first two possibilities because interested and educated readers are familiar with the foreign technical terms. In form-focused texts also explanatory translations are appropriate. Their function is to help the reader in the target language by keeping the foreign term but with a brief appositional supplement relating it to familiar concepts. In this procedure something is always lost, but the information essential to an understanding of the text is preserved without unduly distorting the form of the statement with lengthy circumlocutions. For example, if the Spanish *chacolí* is translated as "Biscayan wine," the Spanish reader misses the identification of a light sharp wine, but the reader in the target language learns that this must be a special kind of wine from a particular region of Spain. If *las Cortes* is translated as "the Spanish Estates Parliament" nothing is said about this particular variety of parliament, but it is probably hinted that this is not a parliament on the Western democratic model. The closer the explanatory element is to the original text and the briefer and more suggestive of the foreign situation it can be, the better.[105] In form-focused texts it is the best way of dealing with place-related factors, because footnotes are a nuisance, breaking the flow of reading and marring the effectiveness of the text in the target language.

---

[105] This concept of explanatory translations requires more precision. It frequently happens, especially with a place-related determinant, that a translation relies on a definition that would be found in a monolingual dictionary, which may produce an effect esthetically worse than a parenthetical statement or a footnote. For example, when the Spanish *alpargatas* ("canvas shoes") is translated as "Schuhwerk aus Hanf in Sandalenform" ("sandal-type footwear made of hemp") the information may be accurate enough, but not the form, and especially in a form-focused text it is the form that should receive priority.

The decision of which of the four possibilities to choose depends very much on the degree to which the sensitivities of the source language can be appreciated in the target language. The more closely two cultures are related to each other and the more that mass media and tourism make different cultures and their distinctive features common knowledge throughout the world, the greater the probability that footnotes and explanatory translations will be unnecessary. With regard to place-related determinants, George Mounin's (1967, p. 108) statement is absolutely true for translators as well as for translation critics, that "in order to translate a language well" – and we would add, in order to evaluate a translation objectively – "it is not enough to learn the language. One must study its culture, not just as an interested visitor, but from the ground up, and ... systematically."

4.5 The audience factor

Before we can discuss the special problems posed by audience-related factors[106] for the linguistic form of an original text and its translation, the term *audience* itself has to be defined. The "audience" is always the reader or hearer of the text in the *source* language. This audience, addressed in the original, must be strictly distinguished from "special audiences" a translator or his clientele might have in mind and which would render irrelevant any general criteria for translation and translation criticism.[107]

Here we consider as determinants only what the author of the original had in mind for his readers when forming the original text

---

[106] E. A. Nida's "cultural context of the source language" corresponds to what we have distinguished here as place- and audience-related determinants. When translating linguistic symbols which are influenced by these and other non-linguistic determinants, it is necessary to consider what Nida calls the "cultural context of the receptor language" if they are to be properly "decoded."

[107] For example, a children's translation of *Don Quixote* or *Gulliver's Travels* would have to meet standards other than those of a translation faithful to the original text of these works. See 4.7 below.

as he did in the source language, and nothing more. Here again the whole social and cultural context (substantially what we call the situational context) is important, but from a different viewpoint than in our discussion of environmental factors, because there it was primarily a concern with the facts and concepts of the source language. The audience factor is apparent in the common idiomatic expressions, quotations, proverbial allusions and metaphors, etc., of the source language. The amount of consideration that audience-related factors demand depends on the type of text. This usually involves a process of decoding. The translator should make it possible for the reader in the target language to see and understand the text in the terms of his own cultural context. The following examples of idiomatic expressions will illustrate the point.

In a content-focused text, for example, the Spanish expression "miente más que el gobierno" ("he lies worse than the government") does not have a strictly literal parallel in German. Since the form of the expression is secondary, and in this type of text it is the content that is to be preserved, a rendering of the semantic value of the expression, such as "he's an awful liar," should serve as an adequate translation. In a form-focused text, however, an idiomatic German expression of similar semantic content would have to be found, because the shape of the expression assumes a position of priority: An adequate translation in this instance would be "er lügt wie gedruckt" ("he lies like a rug," or literally, "he lies like it's printed"). In an appeal-focused text, as in a political campaign or a satire, a more common form of language would be adopted, but with an allusion to something in the immediate historical context to render the Spanish expression. At the time of the Spiegel affair the German translation would have been a literal "er lügt mehr als die Regierung" ("he lies more than the administration"), which would mean nothing to a German reader of another period. There can also be "transposed equivalents" when the target language cannot render the original effect directly due to differences between the languages and compensates by a comparable effect at a different location.

Similar considerations may affect the translation of images in comparisons. In a content-focused text the expression "Etre connu comme le loup blanc" (literally, "to be known like the white wolf") could be translated as "well known," while in a form-focused text some comparable figure would be expected that would reflect the same semantic kernel, be an equally current expression and of similar stylistic level in the target language, such as "bekannt sein wie ein bunter Hund" (literally, "as familiar as a mongrel," i.e., "something everyone knows"). In an appeal-focused text the question becomes why *this* particular image was selected, whether it was for the term *loup* "wolf" or the term *blanc* "white". Then the proper adaptation can be made to preserve the right semantic element depending on the context.

One more example will illustrate the theme of this chapter. Ortega y Gasset (1937, p. 18-19) writes: "Y yo, a mi vez, entreveo que es usted una especie de último abencerraje, último superviviente de una fauna desaparecida, puesto que es usted capaz, frente a otro hombre, de creer que es el otro y no usted quien tiene razón." In the diglot edition this is translated: "Und ich, für meinen Teil, habe das Gefühl, daß Sie eine Art letzter 'Abencerraje' sind, ein letzter Überlebender einer ausgestorbenen Fauna, da Sie einem anderen Menschen gegenüber fähig sind, zu glauben, daß der andere und nicht Sie selbst recht haben" (literally, "And I, for my part, feel that you are something like the last 'Abencerraje,' the last survivor of an extinct species of fauna, since you are capable of believing that others and not you yourself are right").

The generally awkward quality of the translation aside, important here is the phrase "último abencerraje." Assuming that translations are primarily intended for readers who are not familiar with the source language, an allusion in it should never be simply translated if it is unintelligible to a reader in the target language. The meaning of the word 'Abencerraje' can reasonably be inferred from the microcontext ("ein letzter Überlebender" = "a last survivor") as the last example of something. But the macrocontext is completely confusing for the reader who can only deduce that an "Abencerraje" is some kind of animal. The translated text, however, should be just as intelligible as the original. Pictures and comparisons from the world of the audience in the source language have to be carried over into the thought world of the readers in the target language. For the Spaniard "el último abencerraje" is an historical character;[108] "fauna" refers (ironically) to "human beings." An idiomatic rendering would be something like "the last of the Mohicans" (Dornseiff, 1959, p. 32); and in place of "fauna" a term like "race," or "clan" should be used. This is necessary if the translation is to convey an equivalent meaning.

These principles are also good for evaluating a translation. For example, when translating the novel *El Jarama* by Rafael Sánchez Ferlosio, idiomatic phrases drawn from bull fighting such as "Ahí, ya ves, *has estado,*" or "Sabe *dar la salida* como nadie" would make no sense if translated literally for the German reader (Dornseiff, 1959, p. 38). Some would even demand as a critical criterion that the translator develop a special bull fight vocabulary in German in order to "preserve the foreign atmosphere", but thanks to the attractiveness of Spain for German tourists, the German reader today has a good general idea of bull fighting, although the finer points of the artistic value of certain moves may well be unknown. In this instance the critic should recognize common German idioms as match the context in a broader or narrower sense as adequate translations, and translate the former example as "du hast den Nagel auf den Kopf getroffen" ("you've hit the nail on the head"), and the latter as "er versteht sich eben besser darauf als jeder andere" ("he knows how to deal with it better than anyone").

It is the same with the Englishman's love of tea, which leads to a variety of English idiomatic expressions. As F. Güttinger (1963, p. 14) notes, the expression "it isn't my cup of tea" should not be translated as "das ist nicht meine Tasse Tee" simply to preserve an "English atmosphere." Even if the German reader can guess the

---

[108] Muhammad XI (d. 1527), sultan of Granada, the last Moslem stronghold in Spain, conquered in 1492 by the Catholic rulers of Aragon and Castile, Ferdinand and Isabella [Tr.].

meaning of the idiom from its linguistic and situational context,
its very strangeness produces a different effect in a German text.
In English it is a common and ordinary expression, comparable to
the German idiom "das ist nicht mein Fall" (literally, "that is not
my case").

4.6 The speaker factor

By speaker-related determinants we mean primarily those elements
which affect the language of the author himself or of his creation as
extra-linguistic factors. These factors appear in many ways on the
lexical, grammatical and stylistic levels. The extent to which they
should be considered in translating depends again on the particular
type of text represented. They should have the least influence in
content-focused texts, where the words, syntax and style are far more
determined by the subject than by the author. A few exceptions are
commentaries, non-fiction books and feature articles, where the stylistic devices of the author are emulated in the target language to
the extent possible although in distinct subordination to the content
matter. In form-focused texts they are determinative not only for
the style of an author to the extent he is influenced by his origins,
his education and the period he lives in, his relationship to a particular school or tradition (for example, an author of the Romantic
period writes differently than a naturalist author), they are also
critically important for the stylistic "persona" of an author (a wash-
erwoman does not speak like a reporter, nor a child like an adult).
In appeal-focused texts it must further be considered that a particular extra-linguistic, nonliterary purpose affects the vocabulary,
syntax and style of the author in the sense that the mode of the linguistic form is always shaped by the goal of achieving the maximum
effect. Finally, in audio-medial texts, especially in stage plays, the
spoken forms are not subject simply to the laws of spoken syntax
and good dialog structure. As in many form-focused texts, it is
far more important to portray individuals by their language as
members of a particular region (dialect), social level (jargon, col-

loquialisms, standard usage), and professional or even religious group (technical terms). This is ample proof that the influence of speaker-related determinants on the form of a text is sufficient to deserve the attention of both the translator and the critic.

4.7 Affective implications

Emotional determinants affect primarily lexical and stylistic matters, but they extend also to the grammatical level (morphologically as well as syntactically) of the source language version. Charles Bally in another context recognized the significance of this factor for linguistic forms. "For him," George Mounin (1967, p. 87) says, "it was obvious from the beginning that in a language there are 'affective values,' 'means of expression,' 'affective elements of thought,' an 'affective character of means of expression,' an 'affective syntax,' and the like." The critic should test whether these implications are appropriately echoed in the target language. He should notice whether the linguistic means for expressing humor or irony, scorn or sarcasm, excitement or emphasis in the original have been properly recognized by the translator and rendered appropriately in the target language. Frequently the linguistic elements of the original alone do not call sufficient attention to particular affective aspects, so that these must be detected in other ways. Naturally in appeal-focused texts these determinants call for the greatest attention.

A rewarding illustration of this in dealing with German and Spanish is the diminutive form, which abounds in Spanish. The translator cannot be too sensitive to the linguistic variety produced by this morphological element, distinguishing whether the suffix indicates a diminution in objective dimensions or a sign of an affective quality. The precise kind of affective quality can usually be determined from the context, preferably the situational context.[109]

---

[109] See R. Seco (1954, p. 123): "Por lo general, los diminutivos ... presentan una larga escala de matices oscilantes – según la frase, la entonación y los interlocutores – entre el sentido despreciativo, la ironía y la expresión cariñosa ..."

An example from the novel, *Nada,* by Carmen Laforet (1958, p. 117) will illustrate: "¿No te da miedo de andar tan *solita* por las calles? ¿Y si viene el *lobito* y te come?"

With the word "solita" the suffix has an emotional and intensive force. It is impossible to render the *-ita* with a German diminutive, because in German only a substantive can take a diminutive.[110] The emotional and intensive components are best expressed in German by a compound adjective: "mutterseelenallein" ("all on one's own;" thus, "Aren't you afraid to be walking here *all by yourself?*"). Again, with the word "lobito" the suffix "-ito" lacks any belittling or trivializing force. From the situational context it is clear that the girl Andrea is treated affectionately and ironically like an innocent little child. This quality can be expressed by translating the word "lobito" as "And what if the *big bad wolf* comes and eats you?" (Bonse, 1968, p. 106-107).

Swear words also pose a problem for translation: the emotional elements must be carefully matched with the specific situational context. Taken abstractly they can run the gamut of emotional nuances. Only the precisely matching nuance should be struck in the target language. But that is not all! Animal names are known to be favored as swear words, but different languages have different associations for different animals. Most frequently the translator must make some modification if the swear word is to be expressed with its proper effect. When a Frenchman swears at someone with the words "la vache!" the German translation as "Die(se) Kuh!" (literally "the cow!") would miss the meaning completely. Apart from the fact that in German this could only apply to something femi-

---

("In general the diminutives ... offer a wide variety of fluctuating shades – depending on the expression, the intonation and the speakers – ranging from contempt to irony and tender affection ...").

[110] See J. Erben (1966, p. 101): "Eine Diminutivbildung ... erhalten vor allem Bezeichnungen solcher Lebewesen und Dinge, zu denen der Sprecher ein emotionales Verhältnis hat" ("A diminutive form ... is possible primarily for names of beings and things with which the speaker may have an emotional relationship").

nine, the word carries the associations of "stupid" and "awkward," while "la vache" as a swear word finds its equivalent in the German word "Schwein!" (English, "bastard!").

Similarly with the words "hen" and "duck" in English and German. D. MacDermott (1969, p. 61) writes: "... the scarcely less foolish *hen*, at least in Glasgow, may be a friendly way of addressing a young woman, similar to the *duck* or *duckie* heard in England." "Huhn" or "Ente" as a pet name in German would be at the least unusual, so that the shift to "Kätzchen" ("kitty") or "Mäuschen" ("mousie") would be preferable. Exclamations of every kind also need to be tested very carefully before their equivalents in a target language can be pronounced optimal. A. Malblanc (1961, p. 30) offers an interesting example of this: "Du dehors la maison n'avait l'air de rien. Jamais on ne se serait cru devant la demeure d'un héros. Mais quand on y entrait, coquin de sort!" ("From the outside the house was unpretentious. No one would ever believe it was the home of a hero. But on entering the house, what a sight!") (*Tartarin de Tarascon*, p. 2). Malblanc adduced two translations (without naming sources): a) "Von außen hatte das Haus gar nichts so Absonderliches und Außergewöhnliches, und nach diesen äußeren Eindrücken würde man auch niemals auf die Vermutung kommen, daß drinnen ein Held wohnen könne; wenn man das Haus aber betrat, Himmel und die Welt, was gab's da zu sehen!" ("From the outside the house had nothing special or unusual, and from this external impression one would never have the feeling that a hero would live in it; but if one entered the house, heaven and the world, what there was to see!"); b) "Nein, von außen merkte man dem Haus nichts an. Niemad hätte geglaubt, vor der Wohnstatt eines Helden zu stehen. Aber wenn man hineinging: Donnerwetter noch einmal!" ("No, from outside the house was unassuming. No one would believe they stood before a hero's home. But on going in: thunderbolts and double it!").

The expression "coquin de sort!" which is an exclamation of surprise or an acknowledgment of amazement, has been translated once far too amply and explicitly as "Himmel und die Welt, was gab's da zu sehen" (literally, "heaven and the world, what a sight there was!"), and again somewhat ambiguously as "Donnerwetter noch einmal!" ("Thunderbolts! and double it!"). In the first German translation Malblanc rightly notices the lack of Gallic wit. And in his view the second example fails to reflect the "special, delightful resonance" of this "exclamation typical of Provence." The "regional accent" that Malblanc misses could possibly be rendered in German by an expression with a slightly dialect tang, such as "Dunnerkiel" (English, "I say!" or "my word!") in place of "Donnerwetter."

Meanwhile an appreciation of the affective determinants reveals clearly the limits of objective translation criticism. It is almost inevitable that subjectively conditioned differences of interpretation will appear. This makes it the more difficult to achieve an objective judgment, no matter how strictly objective the critic may try to be.

4.8 Extra-linguistic determinants as a pragmatic category of translation criticism

From the above discussion it is evident that a comprehensive evaluation addressing all the factors that influence a translation is impossible if the critic considers only the particular demands of each type of text and the distinctive elements of each language. Frequently the latter can be conclusively interpreted only when the linguistic context is evaluated in the light of its situational context. In other words, the critic must take into consideration the effect of extra-linguistic determinants on the linguistic form of the original text just as thoroughly as the translator must when doing the translating. Especially with regard to affective implications it should be recognized that under certain circumstances the translator and the critic both may consider the effects of these determinants and arrive at different conclusions, so that clearly despite all methodological precautions, a subjective element in criticism cannot be completely ruled out. And yet this qualification in no way calls into question either the justice or the value of translation criticism.

Beside the literary and linguistic categories, the critic has yet a third category available for making an objective judgment. This may finally be called the pragmatic category of translation criticism because it does not rely on linguistic factors of a purely objective nature.

C. The Limitations of Translation Criticism

> Translation and especially the poet is one of the most important functions in a literature, partly because these lead people who have no knowledge of other languages to those forms of humanity and the arts which constitute the peculiar significance of every nation, and which they would never experience otherwise, but also partly and even more significantly because they expand the value and expressiveness of their own language.
>
> W. von Humboldt (1963), Introduction to the translation of *Agamemnon* by Aeschylus

> Anyone who really wants to translate must first of all believe in what he translates.
>
> J. J. Breitinger, *Critische Dichtkunst*

In discussing the limitations of translation criticism, there are two aspects to be distinguished. On the one hand, where does the critic of a target language version find the limits of *translation* criticism, and on the other, just what are the *limits* of translation criticism. The first point is basically concerned with every material deviation from the source text: how much change can there be before it can no longer be called a translation? The second involves subjective perspectives which unavoidably affect objective judgments, limiting the judgment of the critic unintentionally and frequently quite unconsciously.

Thus far we have been discussing the possibility of an objective criticism of translations, analyzing the results of the process under three different categories: a literary category (text types), a language category (linguistic elements), and a pragmatic category (non-linguistic determinants). In the course of the discussion it has been repeatedly noted that these three principal categories need to be supplemented by other perspectives when translation methods vary from the norms. As we shall see, these perspectives may be characterized as functional and personal.

5. Objective and subjective limits of translation criticism

The categories of translation criticism discussed above are based upon factors that govern the translation process under normal circumstances. Neglecting any one of these factors under any circumstances would affect the full equivalence of the source and target texts.

There can be norms only when there can be deviations from a norm. We stated that normally for an adequate translation it is critical to consider carefully a text's type, linguistic elements and non-linguistic determinants. But it should not be ignored that in practice variations from this normal procedure occur when taking a source text into a target language. One very important cause of objective differences from the source text is a disregard for its text type. This always occurs when the translation is intended for a special function. If the special function has to do with the subject matter, the purpose of the translation may be something other than that of the original; if it has to do with persons, the translation may be addressed to a different readership than the original.

In such instances the translator may be as independent of the principles of the text type, the observance of linguistic elements and the consideration of non-linguistic determinants as the purpose or the intended readership of the translation may require. The critic must then accommodate the intended function of the translation among the criteria for its evaluation. The literary, linguistic and pragmatic categories of translation criticism will be replaced by a *functional* category.

It remains a question, of course, as to whether this functional category should be recognized as useful in translation criticism. It can hardly be regarded as reducing the possibility of objective criticism in general – at most it indicates a limitation of *translation* criticism. But this is enough to qualify the functional category for inclusion in a chapter on the limits of translation criticism.

The real debate can only be on whether versions in a target language should or should not be considered translations if they serve a particular purpose, especially a purpose *not* addressed by the original. Whenever the translation does not serve the purpose intended in the original it strays from the ideal of a translation in the strict sense, whether the motivation be artistic (e.g., a change of form, as in dramatic presentations of epic poems, prose versions of dramatic works, etc.), pedagogical (student editions, interlinear versions), or commercial (rough drafts, adaptations). In other words, just how broadly or how narrowly should the concept of translation be construed? But this is an old debate that has been decided variously through the centuries (Kloepfer, 1967, chs. 1 and 3; Wuthenow, 1969, chs. 1 and 2).

By the term *translation* we mean here the version of a source text in a target language where the primary effort has been to reproduce in the target language a text corresponding to the original as to its textual type, its linguistic elements, and the non-linguistic determinants affecting it. On the surface this definition excludes any consideration of translations which do not share the purpose of the original or have a purpose other than that of the original author, and are directed to the interests of a special clientele. Such products are better characterized as adaptations, paraphrases, more or less free revisions, abstracts, summaries, and the like.

As we have emphasized elsewhere, there is no question of the basic legitimacy or usefulness of making adaptations of original texts, but it would be better to call them "adaptations" – or more or less free adaptations – and not translations. This slight change of terminology would clearly imply substantive changes in a target language version without implying any evaluative judgment.

The criticism of "*adaptations*" cannot be held to a consistent observation of the criteria and categories appropriate to translation criticism. The critic must instead determine whether the transformation has achieved the special purpose for which it was intended. The judgment becomes one of a functional category.

A second factor which is subjective rather than objective in nature can give rise to considerable differences between an original work and a target language version. It has to do with the individuality of the translator, which inevitably leaves its imprint on the translation. There can hardly be any two translations of the same text, whatever kind of text it may be, that are similar in all their details, and consequently identical. Wilhelm von Humboldt (1963, p. 97) refers explicitly to these subjective differences and their peculiar characteristics when he states that "the part of the nation that cannot read the ancient classics for themselves can become better acquainted with them through several translations than through just one. They are just so many different views of the same spirit, each translator reflecting his own understanding as he was able to express it – while the reality is found only in the original." Such subjective differences can, of course, be of pedagogical value, provided several versions of the same text are available.

On closer inspection this subjective factor shows two components. First there is the interpretive skill of the translator, where the translator's grasp of a topic is affected by the subjective limitations of the hermeneutical process. This applies to all varieties of text types. The second component involves the individual personality of the translator, where translating may be viewed as a personal problem. This also applies to all text types, but it affects most seriously the translation of literary texts, especially poetry, because only too often the quality of a translator's artistic temperament can lead to radical alterations of the original work. Translations of literary works would better be called free renderings than translations, especially when the personality of the translator and the force of his own artistic temperament result in a target language version that stands on its own, indebted to the original as a model and a source of inspiration.

Differences from the original due to this second factor – the interpretive skill and personality of the translator – take translation criticism to its absolute *limits*, because the critic is also subject to the same conditions. At this point a judgment can no longer be objectively expressed in terms such as "correct" or "false," "good" or "bad." E. A. Nida (1964, p. 164) has stated the situation quite prudently: "One cannot, therefore, state that a particular translation is good or bad without taking in consideration a myriad of factors, which in turn must be weighted in a number of different ways, with appreciably different answers. Hence there will always be a variety of valid answers to the question, 'Is this a good translation?'"

If the translator's work is obviously not directly based on a given text or document, the question "Is this a good translation?" is no longer in order. At the most the translator's interpretation can be compared and weighed with that of the critic; in the case of free rendering the esthetic principles of each can be compared and the way in which artistic views have been worked out in the source and target languages can be reviewed.

But whether differences from the original text are due to objective or subjective conditions, there is one thing that the critic must consider: the criteria and categories of normal translation criticism are no longer adequate. The motives which prompted the translator to change either the form or the content of the original must also be discovered, as well as their implications for the version in the target language. If the translator has not discussed his own motives in a preface or an epilogue, the critic must try and detect them; only then can his criticism claim to achieve the highest degree of objectivity.

Now that the framework for determining the limits of translation criticism have been defined, we will examine in turn the significance of the functional and personal categories for translation criticism.

6. The special function of a translation

As noted before, the functional category is the guiding principle for judging renderings which are designed to serve a special purpose, and are accordingly intended to fulfill a specific function that is not addressed in the original. Under these conditions the appropriateness of a translation method should be judged in the light of the special purpose instead of by the text type.

6.1 *Resumés and summaries*

The first to be noted here are resumés and summaries. This group includes analyses and summaries which appear in daily and trade newspapers and in scientific journals to report only the essential results or particular details of interest to a client. A large number of translators in the diplomatic service, in government offices, in commerce and industry, and in research centers need to master this genre. Here again a translation technique is an indispensable prerequisite; the resultant form in the target language, however, is not determined by the type or kind of text but by the purpose of providing the client with information about an essential content or aspects of it that are of particular interest in a brief, terse and attractive form. Similarly, for the contents of a foreign language novel or play the purpose is to present only as much of the original work as is necessary for a publisher or a theater to decide whether to proceed with a translation or a production. For such transformations the translator needs to understand the essential content sufficiently to summarize its gist and express it in the target language in a normal and fluent style. Fluency in the translation, which in most other instances is a lesser virtue, becomes in this case a positive value for the critic, in contrast to the negative value of translations where the texts are difficult in the original and where skillfully designing a "smooth legibility" amounts to rendering them glib.[111] If resumés

---

[111] See E. Tabernig de Pucciarelli (1964, p. 150): "Si la lectura de Kant no es fácil en su propria lengua, ¿por qué ha de serlo en la versión española? Por eso conservó [el traductor García Morente] la dificultad inherente al filósofo alemán manteniendo detalles al parecer insignificantes, que entorpecen la comprensión y que hacen penosa la lectura. García Morente estaba seguro que toda soltura o facilidad en el decir añadidas a la traducción habrían desvirtuado el original" ("If Kant is not easy reading in his own language, why should it be easy in a Spanish translation? This is why [the translator García Morente] retained

and summaries report the essential content of the original, or represent the details intended by the translator in an acceptable style in the target language, they should be judged both adequate and proper.

6.2 *Rough translations*

Rough translations of poems such as Goethe made use of in his *West-östlicher Divan* are examples of transformations that fulfill a special function. In that instance the translation from the Persian by the German orientalist Josef von Hammers made no claims to literary quality (Güttinger, 1963, p. 34). What Friedhelm Kemp (1965, p. 16f) calls "free rendering" in discussing translations of poetry falls under this rubric. In this connection Kemp defines "free renderings" as "renderings ... which seek to save the outward form at all costs, even at the expense of all that makes for grace, power and originality." Such a formal fidelity may be feasible in languages that are structurally related and share a common cultural heritage, including "a common stock of metrical forms and rhetorical images," for a good translation to reproduce the forms meticulously in a form-focused text (1965, p. 17). But if there is little or no close relationship between the languages, as in the instance of Persian and German poetry, any attempt to reproduce the forms meticulously would produce what we call here a rough translation.

Furthermore, raw translations of theatrical works which are then thoroughly revised for dramatic presentation by a playwright or dramatic editor, also belong here. In this instance the translator is simply asked to provide a literal translation. A critic who complains that such a translation is superficial, neglecting the deeper aspects, or that it does not preserve this or that, lays himself open to the charge of ignoring the purpose of the translation in making the judgment:

---

the inherent difficulty of the German philosopher, keeping details that seemed insignificant, numbing the mind and making reading a chore. García Morente was confident that any smoothness or fluency added in the translation would only distort the original").

the criticism violates the principle of objective relevance.

6.3 *School and study editions*

In our discussion of criteria for judging translations of theatrical works we noted that the translation method used, and consequently the standard for judging them, must be adapted to the purpose of the translations. If the translations are for stage productions, their (audio-medial) text type dictates that priority be assigned to considerations of oral delivery, acting, and dramatic effectiveness (including the interplay of the text with visual and acoustic elements) (Buschkiel, 1966, Mai 5, pp. 51, 52). But if the translation is for school or study editions of dramatic works, the function of the translation (in contrast to the stage orientation of the original text) justifies the use of a translation method designed for form-focused texts. The result of such a translation should not be disqualified by dramatic critics as useless simply because they are ill adapted to stage delivery. Such criticisms would not be objective, because they ignore the function of the translation.

6.4 *Bible translations*

The many kinds of Bible translations provide another example of how the purpose of a translation affects translation methods. If the Bible is translated basically for missionary purposes (as it primarily is when it is first translated into a language), it should be regarded as an appeal-focused text. Luther's translation method is the best in this regard. Goethe understood Luther's version of the Bible in this sense, and insisted that by translating the book consisting of such different styles as from a single mold he "did more to promote the religion than had he tried to preserve the individuality of each part of the original." And Goethe (1962, p. 47) continued, "Since then many have attempted in vain to give us the book of Job, the Psalms and other songs more effectively in their poetical forms. But for the people it was intended for, a simple, smooth translation is still the best."

Only the intention of the Luther translation to serve a mission-ary purpose gives the critic the right to regard positively the fact that it appears to be cast from a single mold, even though this meant leveling the differences between the various text types.

The German translation of the Scriptures by Buber and Rosen-zweig represents an almost diametrically opposite approach. Their translation follows an avowedly different goal. They attempted to render the poetry, the momentum, the expressiveness of the He-brew text in the target language in a way that would preserve the sacred character of the original text; consequently the Bible was for them a form-focused text: "The content cannot be transmitted apart from its form. It is impossible to distinguish what is said from the way it is said," Rosenzweig (1926, pp. 33, 40) wrote, and further on he added, "And if we believe the possibility exists that some day, in its own time or in our time, the word of God can be re-vealed, not just in prescribed dogma, but fundamentally everywhere in human speech, then the translator has the responsibility to repro-duce as faithfully as possible in his own language the specific nuances of the human expression of that revelation, whether by imi-tation or by intimation." Martin Buber (1963, p. 351) expressed himself similarly:

> Even the most important translations of the Scriptures avail-able to us, whether the Greek version of the Septuagint, the Latin of Jerome, or the German of Martin Luther, do not attempt to achieve the original character of the Book in its vocabulary, its syntax and rhythmical structure. In order to make intelligible to a modern community ... a trusted cov-enantal document, they transpose the 'content' of the text into another language, not blatantly abandoning its cha-racteristic elements, structure and dynamic, but yet not attempting to preserve them whenever the 'form' would seem to obstruct the smooth rendering of the content.

A similar distinction between translation methods, based on the stated purposes of the process, prompted E. A. Nida's (1964, p. 160) contrast between "formal correspondence" and "dynamic equivalence." He illustrated this by the biblical passage Romans 16:16: "Salutate invicem in osculo sancto." The formal equivalent in English, according to Nida, is "Greet one another with a holy kiss" (RSV). This retains the cultural situation of the source text. The "dynamic equivalent" according to Nida is "Give one another a hearty handshake all around." This reflects the cultural situation of the readers in the target language. This process can be significant or even necessary if the Bible is considered a missionary (i.e., appeal-focused) text. The present example apparently goes beyond the limits of necessity because the proposed dynamic equivalent trivializes the expression. The text loses its character as sacred text, which should be retained despite its special purpose. Nida himself stresses this point elsewhere: "Religious communication, however, involves certain special difficulties, since it appears to require language having a solemn or esoteric flavor. Such a flavor is often developed by means of archaisms, which, by virtue of their antique appearance, seem to provide the text with a temporally derived authority" (Nida, 1964, p. 222). This can carry over into the cultural situation. With sacred texts the cultural situation in the target language community can assume the priority, especially if it is impossible to understand the text without the additional aid of a preacher or an experienced exegete.

After this necessary excursus it must be stated in summary that for a critic there is generally not the least significance in playing one translation against another (for instance, Luther against Buber-Rosenzweig), calling one "good" and the other "poor." An evaluation can be objective only if the critic takes into consideration the function intended by the translator. The Greek Septuagint, the Latin translation by Jerome (the Vulgate) and Luther's German translation, as first translations in a new language, were primarily intended for missionary use and consequently employed the appeal-focused translation method with all that it implies. A new translation in a language, in contrast, can give greater consideration to the wealth of literary forms in the source, employing the principles for the translation of form-focused texts. These alternative translations may

sometimes offer substantive insights which the earlier formulations
have lost by becoming clichés through long and familiar usage.

The above comments about the Bible naturally apply *mutatis
mutandis* to all sacral texts, and especially to the basic texts of a
religion, with regard to the translation methods of first and later
translations.

6.5 Transformation in literary works

The peculiar character of Luther's translation of the Bible leads to
another example. Quite often poetical works are rendered as prose
in target languages. Renderings of this kind may be fully justified.
There can be many reasons for a translator to opt for a modified
form of standard translation procedures. Objective grounds such as
a certain inflexibility of the target language, a degree of reluctance
for it to accommodate foreign forms of expression (Merian-
Genast, 1958, p. 35), and the structural incompatibility of the source
and target languages, could move a translator to decide between a
poetical rendering and a more normal prose form. But subjective
motives could be operative equally as well, such as a desire to express the content of the foreign poem most powerfully without
having to observe the restrictive demands of emulating or even
taking into consideration its artistic form.

Such motivations – and especially subjective motivations[112] –
must be considered in making an evaluation, whether or not the
critic believes they are valid. Here again the *function* of a translation is critical as a category for translation criticism.

---

[112] See the view represented by Goethe in *Dichtung und Wahrheit* (Goethe,
1926, vol. 24, p. 47): "I give due honor to both rhythm and rhyme, which are
the primary characteristics of poetry as poetry, but the most profound and vital
component, the formative and stimulating element, is what remains of the poet
when it is translated into prose. That is the pure and perfect substance: frequently when it is lacking a brilliant facade will feign it, and when it is present,
conceal it."

6.6 Interlinear versions

The so-called interlinear versions also belong here, because they are renderings with a specific purpose. By interlinear versions is not meant simply the primitive literal translations which, as Franz Rosenzweig remarked,[113] in every nation characterize the beginnings of translation activities, and which is practiced by beginners even today – a procedure used as a teaching aid showing a variety of preliminary stages before the final formulation of a text in a target language. Rather what is meant is primarily a word-for-word translation sometimes used in grammars and textbooks for learning a foreign language, where the line translating each individual word is written immediately below the foreign language text. Also included is what Friedhelm Kemp (1965, p. 21) calls in this connection "a transfer in the narrow sense," namely "a kind of impossible translation." Kemp defines this "transfer in the narrow sense" as "a more or less interpretive version which is literal and metrically correct to the extent of sacrificing formal aspects and ignoring rhyme schemes. It preserves syntactical structures, keeps illustrations undistorted, and retains word associations. As an interlinear version it is unflatteringly faithful, leading a shadowy existence and never appearing without the original it serves."

Interlinear versions of this kind can be properly evaluated only in terms of their function. Their only justification lies in being an aid to reading and understanding a foreign language text for purposes of instruction and study, primarily intended for beginners as a valuable guide to a better appreciation of the foreign language or to a more intimate understanding of the original text. If an interlinear version achieves this function it deserves a positive evaluation, even if the linguistic form differs from or even flaunts the laws and norms of the target language – which under the circumstances can hardly be avoided.

---

[113] F. Rosenzweig (1926, p. 17): "There is a quite typical sequence in the history of translating. First there is the simple positioning of translations between the lines designed to assist in reading the original ...."

6.7 Scholarly translations

The criticism of so-called scholarly translations should be treated
similarly, as they are closely related to interlinear versions both in
their method and in their function. Fritz Güttinger (1963, p. 28ff)
uses this term to characterize translations representing a translation
method advocated by Schleiermacher and by Ortega y Gasset after
him. Schleiermacher (1963, p. 39ff) is known to contrast *interpreting* (dolmetschen: workaday, utilitarian translating) with *translating*
(übersetzen: of more sophisticated focus). Translations "of a purely
narrative or descriptive kind" and translations "of newspaper articles and normal travel accounts" are "the province of the *interpreter*,"
while the operations of "the *translator*, in the strict sense, are in the
areas of science and the arts." Schleiermacher (1963, p. 47) accordingly developed his famous alternatives with regard to translation
methods: "Either the translator leaves the author as undisturbed
as possible and requires the reader to be adaptable, or he makes
no demands on the reader and requires the author to be adaptable."
He does not permit a third possibility or a compromise between
the two methods. This possibility was not seen until later, and
meanwhile "instead of a negative and divisive either/or," a fully
"positive both/and approach was developed" (Kloepfer, 1967, p.
69). Obviously the first of Schleiermacher's alternatives proposes
the "scholarly" translation, where the reader must recognize the foreignness of the author. He has to learn new thoughts and new
expressions he has never met before, "and himself become the foreigner, no longer at home" (Merian-Genast, 1958, p. 25). Ortega y
Gasset's (1937, p. 88-89) demands go yet further: he wishes "the
translated author's idiosyncracies to be mirrored in the translation,
even to the extreme limits of intelligibility."

The function of such scholarly translations is to make it easier
for the interested scholarly reader in the target language who lacks
any knowledge (or at least a sufficient knowledge) of the source
language to penetrate the spirit and imagination of a world that is
foreign to his own language, and acquaint him with unfamiliar

esthetic principles, artistic perspectives and experiences. Güttinger (1963, p. 30; examples p. 30f) suggests that "anyone who wishes to study a piece of foreign literature without mastering its language will find that the best tool is a most literal rendering of its form and matter." But then, if "the grammatical tolerance" of the target language is "forced to its limits," as Ortega y Gasset praises the German translations of his works for having done, it would be no surprise if the effect of such a translation seems correspondingly distorted or "forced." Scholarly translations have their own justification, as we have noted, but as Ortega y Gasset (1937, p. 86-87) himself has remarked, "the reader should be fully aware that from a literary standpoint that he is not reading a literary gem so much as employing a rather tortuous tool." In this sense a scholarly translation will always leave the fastidious reader unsatisfied. But the dissatisfaction that is felt can also be productive. It may arouse a curiosity and an interest in the original work, and inspire an effort to find the same thoughts expressed more effectively and perhaps more gracefully. But it is only the original that fully combines the thought content integrally with a linguistic form.

The critic's evaluation should also consider the function of the scholarly translation as a quarry for knowledge and instruction and not as a form for literary enjoyment and entertainment. Then the adaptation may not appear so negatively off-putting or be condemned as "unreadable" and "unpalatable." Instead it should take a clue from Ortega y Gasset's (1937, p. 78-79) claim that "the translation is something special, distinct from all other literary categories, with its own standards and purposes, for the simple reason that a translation is not the work itself, but serves as an approach to the work."

7. Specially targeted reader groups

As we have already indicated, the functional category is the category of choice for translation critics if the translator or his client specifies a more restricted group of readers for the target language

version than would normally be addressed by a translation. It should
be clearly understood that this kind of situation is exceptional. And
for this reason we must dissent from Theodore H. Savory's views
when he makes the audience addressed by a translation a guide-
line for the translation method to be adopted. From Savory's (1958,
p. 26) perspective four kinds of audience may be distinguished.
1. Readers who are ignorant of the original language and are interested only in literary content. For these a *free* translation is right,
and it goes without saying that any kind of translation criticism is
irrelevant. 2. Readers who are interested in learning the language
of the original and wish to increase their familiarity with it partly
through relevant literature in translation. For these the *most literal*
translations are best. But then the question is whether this does not
amount to misleading the readers. The *language* of the originals is
far better learned by reading the originals themselves. If the interest
is in familiarity with the *literature* of the language before gaining
an adequate command of the language, the "most literal" translations can hardly be useful, because they can only give a pale and
possibly distorted view of the literary and esthetic value of the original work. Only if the "most literal" translation is used as a crutch
(to avoid having to refer constantly to dictionaries and grammars)
can it serve as a useful tool. But then it qualifies as an interlinear
version, and the critic should evaluate it as such (Savory, 1958, p.
99f). 3. Readers who once knew the language of the original and
have forgotten it. These, according to Savory, want a translation
that can be recognized as a translation. This is obviously anoma-
lous and unrealistic. On the one hand these may be readers who do
not know the language and want to study it in a translation which
will give them a mirror image of it structures and turns of expression; what they want is a "scholarly" translation, and it is irrelevant
whether they are familiar with the original language or not (Savory,
1958, p. 100f). On the other hand they may wish to renew their
knowledge of the language. Such readers would hardly be helped
by translations; at most they could use interlinear versions as learning and reading aids. 4. Specialists who are familiar with the original
language. These, according to Savory, want translations where su-

perior competence overcomes the limitations of translation. Yet this would seem to be a goal common to all translations, and in no way peculiar to readers who are specialists.

Of course this does not mean that normally translations are not made with a particular group of readers in mind, but rather that in the following examples the groups are usually more clearly and sharply defined. And it should be emphasized once more that the readership envisaged by the original need not remain the same for a translation, but rather it depends directly on the purpose of the translator or his client. In other words, a specially designated readership is one which is sharply distinguished from the normal readers of the original and its translation.

7.1 Editions for children and youth

Translations of children's books are naturally intended to be read by children. This relationship to children provides a criterion for their evaluation. But if a world class story such as *Don Quixote*, *Gulliver's Travels*, *Robinson Crusoe* or *Pinocchio* is translated for children, the version in the target language has to be "revised" or "adapted" for its special reading group. This kind of adaptation would be better called a free rendering, a revision or a paraphrase, depending on how much the content and the form of the original are changed. There is obviously translation work involved, but with many kinds of modification – abbreviations, omissions, simplifications, shifts of emphasis, etc. The result of the translation process can no longer be called a translation in the strict sense. Consequently the normal criteria and categories of criticism can no longer apply. Instead, an objective and fair evaluation must determine whether the work achieves its stated purpose, which in this instance would be adapting the original to very young readers, however this may be understood.

7.2 Popularizations of specialized literature

The situation is somewhat similar in attempts to make the results of scientific research available to interested laymen. These adaptive translations have the purpose of transposing precise technical literature into the everyday idiom of a target language. To this end technical terminology is largely replaced by common words. The dull, long-winded style so often characteristic of scientific literature is abandoned. Not only may passages (of too intricate details) be omitted or abridged, but information may be interpolated and explanations added. All this in the interests of making the original intelligible to a wider circle of readers than was addressed by the original in the source language.

Here again it would be useless to apply normal criteria and categories of translation criticism. Instead the critic must weigh the adaptations and (free) revisions in the light of the functional category to determine whether the adaptive translation is effective in performing the desired function for its intended audience.

In this connection it needs to be restated that adaptive translations cannot be simply equated with translations; the readers of an adaptive translation are not the same ones addressed by the original. If the original is a popularizing presentation, the translation should be measured by the rules and standards which are applied to translations in the strict sense; the critic should judge the result by normal criteria. It is only the *popularizing* target language version of a *technical* original that qualifies for evaluation by the *functional* category of translation criticism.

7.3 Moral, religious, ideological and commercial censorship

Finally we should take notice of adaptive translations (adaptations, revisions) where the foreign original is "purified" for its readers in conformity with certain moral, religious or ideological sensitivities, convictions or values. This kind of revision, prompted often enough by purely commercial interests, is not at all rare. The translator's modifications of the original, whether by expansions, euphemisms, attenuations or omissions, are invariably intended to purify or cleanse the original in the interests of a particular group of readers. Anything in the original which might offend the moral code, the religious feelings or the ideological positions of the intended readers is eliminated; texts may even be altered when necessary and supplementary material added to accommodate the readers.[114]

7.4 Special groups and special functions as a functional category for translation criticism

All three kinds of adaptive translations (for children and youth, popularizing and censored) engage in what may be called (in plain language) a falsification of the original text, because in the target language version the aim of the translator or his client is not that of the original author, and it may possibly be one from which the author would have distanced himself. It should be the obvious responsibility of the translator to disclose the nature of the work as an adaptation, a revision or an adaptive translation. The translator should do this for his own protection against possible charges of incompetence, carelessness or stupidity. The critic would then be duly warned not to evaluate the work by normal standards, but by the criteria for the functional category of translation criticism.

The same applies to the special functions first mentioned above that enable an adaptive translation to achieve its purpose. One can no more enumerate all the various functions than one can count all the different parties they serve. But the examples given here are sufficient to show clearly something of the variety encompassed by the functional category. Ideally in this kind of literature the translator, or in the case of magazines the publisher, should give the reviewer or critic some clue as to how it should be viewed, objectively and functionally.

---

[114] One of the most absurd examples of this was in the Spanish dubbing of foreign films in the 1950s, when censorship required lovers to be called aunts or sisters. By far the best known example would be the many translations of the *Arabian Nights*.

8. Subjective limits of translation criticism

In concluding it remains to address the limitations of translation criticism. Here again we cannot avoid the need to begin by examining more closely the translation process itself once more.

8.1 The hermeneutical process as subjectively conditioned

There is no question that simply reading a text sets in motion an act of interpretation. By this we do not mean just the necessity for an interpretation such as R. L. Politzer refers to. Politzer has in mind the decisions the translator faces when the original text provides no clues. As an example he points to languages which have no generic word for "horse," but only specific words for white, dark, young, male or female horses, or which have not only singular and plural numbers but also a dual number. "How can you translate 'my children,'" he asks, "if the original text does not distinguish between, 'two and more than two?' You interpret and become more precise than the text you are translating" (Politzer, 1966, p. 34).

What concerns us here is not simply the interpretation of different lexical and grammatical structures where the translator has to make clear and definite decisions in the target language, but rather interpretation in the broadest sense based on an appreciation of the text as a whole, namely the hermeneutical process which is involved in the simple reading (or hearing) of any text. This process decides primarily what the reader infers from a text or reads into it. Every translator is also first a reader of the text which will become the material for translation. From this it follows that a translator who takes his work seriously and considers it his responsibility to communicate without any prejudice the thoughts, perspectives, arguments, intentions and purposes of the text's author, will not try to adapt the text to his own taste or perspective but will be mindful of his responsibility as a mediator even as he reads, and he will read with discernment, observing the inherent principles established from the start as common to all translation activity. Ultimately every analysis admittedly issues in an interpretation, no matter how objective one tries to be. Yet it still remains the best counsel for the translator to "feel himself in the position of the original author."

This means that *every* translation is necessarily also an interpretation. Of course the possibility and the necessity for similarities as well as differences between various translations of the very same original is due among other reasons to the fact that the translator – as distinct from the interpreter – works from a fixed written text which is unable to convey the speech mannerisms and intonations of the author, and as Hans-Georg Gadamer[115] emphasizes, can therefore be more ambiguous than the spoken word. Even more significant is the "tentative nature" of translations, because every translator is an interpreter. When Gadamer (1998, p. 365) says that "the foreignness of a language is simply an extreme example of a hermeneutical difficulty, i.e., of foreignness and its resolution," he is focusing on the intrinsic nature of the process. And it should also be added that limitations may also be personal: ultimately interpretations will stand or fall with the interpreter. Personal character, historical setting in time and space, and degree of facility with languages (both source and target languages) as well as educational level achieved are subjective limitations to the effectiveness of interpreters, leading them in particular directions and making their decisions favor their *own* understandings and preferences in what and how they translate. It is a commonly accepted fact that it is impossible to preserve *all* the values of the original in a translation. It is also a truism that in translating a choice must at times be made between two or more possibilities. A first decision, which is based on interpretation, leads to a second decision on how the results of the interpretation may best be represented in the target language. And this again has its

---

[115] H. G. Gadamer (1998, p. 371): "Gesprochenes Wort legt sich in erstaunlichem Grade von selber aus, durch die Sprechweise, den Ton, das Tempo usw ..." ("The spoken word is amazingly self-interpretive through intonation, accent, timing, etc ...").

subjective aspects. Even when two translators are in complete agreement on the interpretation of a text or a passage, their translations in a target language will almost never be identical. Their choices of optimal equivalents from among all the potential equivalents in the language are so influenced by non-linguistic factors that only rarely is the same equivalent chosen. However objective they may try to be, in the end the choice will be subjective, because it is influenced by factors over which the translators have no control and from which they cannot, even with the best of intentions, disengage themselves. These have to do with belonging to a particular nation sharing a particular language and culture. Ideally, given the identical interpretation, the form of a version in German as the target language would be quite different depending on whether the translator is a Swiss, Austrian or German – or even a North, West, South or East German (quite independently of political affiliations). Similar subjective factors would include a person's educational level and personal habits of speech and style.

The range of variation and possibilities of interpretation would differ in the various text types and kinds of texts. They would be fewer in content-focused texts than in form-focused texts; in appeal-focused texts the differences would be greater than in form-focused texts but still fewer than in audio-medial texts. Again, within the content-focused text type of a philosophical nature there would be a greater range of differences than in newspaper articles or bibliographical surveys, etc. Among form-focused texts there would be a greater variety of interpretation in lyrical poems than in short stories or novels, etc.

All the factors enumerated here, whether the presuppositions of an interpretation or the decisions made in translating, may be considered as subjective factors affecting the hermeneutical process.

These factors naturally also affect the critic of a translation. Ultimately the demand that critics not assume the role of judges is essentially grounded in the very human subjectivity which characterizes both the translator and the critic. This subjective condition of the hermeneutical process also makes the further demand that a critic should give reasons for his judgment, whether it be positive or negative, and in the end, following the suggestion of A. W. von Schlegel (1963, p. 99) cited earlier, "there should always be a proposed remedy" whenever a negative judgment is rendered.

In other words, sweeping statements such as "superbly translated," "awkwardly translated," "a sympathetic translation," etc., as well as such radically censorial expressions as "false" or "true" should be eliminated from translation criticisms. It is far better to agree with Julius Wirl (1958, p. 39) that "the farther ... the elements of a text or the text as a whole stays from material specifics or analytical reasoning, the more varied its influence may be with readers and hearers, ... and the less likely a particular translation (paraphrase or rendering) can be shown to be the best or accepted as uniquely true." Such judgments as "true" and "false" are pertinent only when grammatical or typographical errors show a translator to be either lacking competence in the language or simply irresponsible.

8.2 The translator's personality

A consistent appreciation of the personal category of translation criticism should replace sweeping judgments and petty criticisms. This would not only give recognition to the subjective conditions of the hermeneutical process, but also what is actually involved: the personality of the translator and how it affects the translation in the target language.[116] Frequently a critic can appreciate the interpretation of a translator with whom he disagrees only by taking the

---

[116] Examples of the critical influence of the translator's personality and of the understanding and objectives of translation characteristic of the person and his period may be found in R.- R. Wuthenow (1969, p. 19-24) where Shakespeare's 18th sonnet together with translations by Gottlob Regis, Otto Gildemeister, Friedrich Bodenstedt, Stefan George, R. A. Schröder and Karl Kraus are the subject of a very sensitive analysis. "It appears that while each of the versions is more or less related to the original, each in its apparent and approximate degree of 'accuracy' represents the original to an extent, but not completely."

personality of the translator into consideration.

What do we mean by personality in the connection? Since its establishment as a branch of science, characterology has sought to formulate a basic typology for understanding and distinguishing the various kinds of human character. According to a comprehensive survey by Paul Hellwig (1936), competing typologies range from those with no claims on systematic discipline to recent scientific and medically specialized models. For our purposes the scientific typology developed by Eduard Spranger (1920) may serve best. In the chapter on "Basic forms of individuality" Spranger distinguishes six different forms of personality. These forms are 1. theoretical, 2. economic, 3. esthetic, 4. social, 5. aggressive, and 6. religious.

Without anticipating the results of any intensive research in the relations between basic personality types and translating, a few observations are necessary for a more complete definition of the "personal category" of translation criticism, and to develop some criteria that will foster greater objectivity in translation criticism. Of course, it should be remembered that as Hellwig notes, Spranger "does not start from actual behavior and types, but from conceptual analysis," and consequently his types are "basically ... abstractions." And translators do not represent a single "ideal type" but rather a variety of actual complex personalities. Even Spranger himself in a later publication on his eightieth birthday explained that his basic types never claimed to be photo reproductions of actual life, but only point to a particular mind-set or tendency as *dominant* in an individual's personality. And it is this aspect of dominance in a translator's personality that is important for our present discussion.

At this point for heuristic purposes it may be inferred that the aggressive type, characteristically "egocentric, self-assertive, vital and vigorous," is ill adapted to be a translator (Hellwig, 1936, p. 84). The attitude fundamental to a translator is a willingness to empathize freely and fully with an author's original work, with its statements, expressions, form and intention. An essentially aggressive person, even with the best of intellectual and philosophical motives, would hardly be expected to fit this mold. Whether intentionally or not, his translation in a target language would more or less mutilate the author's original, treating it more like raw material for reworking from his own perspective than as a text to be treated considerately and rendered with fidelity. In general an aggressive person would hardly be inclined to undertake translating, because for all its importance and creative potential, translating is primarily an act of service.

The theoretical type, characterized by Spranger (1920, p. 82) as "one who avoids subjectivity, is ideally dispassionate and objective," would be especially good in translating technical works, and philosophical works in particular, because understanding and dealing with things rationally is his forte. He is, so to speak, completely objective, completely elemental, completely generic, completely rational. But in an attempt to translate works of creative literature or poetry he would feel utterly frustrated, because his predominantly theoretical character would not only prevent him from producing creative or artistic work, but probably also make it impossible for him to have an adequate appreciation of the artistic and esthetic aspects of an original work.

The economic type is characterized primarily by a utilitarian view of life. For Spranger "he views development as a series of choices and adaptations which should be exploited to one's advantage. All of life is for him a kind of test of wits." Accordingly the economic type is the best qualified to translate appeal-focused texts as well as content-focused and appeal-focused audio-medial texts, while being less well suited to translate form-focused texts.

And finally the esthetic type, who according to Spranger is "one for whom all *im*pressions become *ex*pressions," (Hellwig, 1936, p. 83) is unquestionably the best translator of form-focused texts, and particularly of literary, poetical and audio-medial texts with form-focused tendencies. His special qualification lies in his pronounced talent for artistic and esthetic values. On the other hand his artistic understanding and esthetic principles may frequently affect the form of his "translation." When this happens the critic should not fault the translation as "wrong" or "useless" on the basis of a strict comparison of texts. Instead in his review he should attempt to recognize the difference between the "artistic temperament" of the author and that of the translator, and show how it affects the target language version. On occasion he may conclude that while the different artistic temperament of the translator has led to a number of changes from the original, it may also have improved the quality of the translation.[117]

It is no accident that translations which have achieved independent status as masterpieces represent peaks in the turbulent history of translation – think of Goethe's *Life of Benvenuto Cellini*, Schlegel's translations of Shakespeare's plays, Tieck's version of *Don Quixote* (which is a masterpiece despite its demonstrable flaws in translation), Rilke's translation of 24 sonnets by Louize Labé,[118] the translations of Baudelaire by Stefan George (Kemp, 1965, p. 25f).

As we noted above, when the artistic temperament and esthetic views of the translator do not coincide with those of the original author, it might be better to speak of free renderings rather than of translations. Free renderings would then also refer to instances where, besides differences in artistic temperament and the translator's esthetic ideas, the source and target languages are divided by essentially incompatible structures and formal elements. A translation beleaguered by such challenges can at best offer "a more or less free use, rearrangement, or reorientation of the original to its own new purpose" as dictated by the differences between the two languages (Kemp, 1965, p. 17). Friedhelm Kemp calls this kind of translation a form of "re-composing" (Umdichtung), not least because the range of changes from the original involved here is far greater than in target language versions characterized as free ren-

---

[117] R. Borchardt (1920, p. 354) wrote: "The author who translates can only translate as he writes: he does not reproduce a work of art, but reacts to the echoes he hears, spontaneously responding to the shapes he sees and the outlines of their forms."

[118] See H. Friedrich (1965, p. 12ff) and his critique of the translation of these sonnets.

derings. In any event, a poet-translator is creative when dealing with the work of a poet in a foreign language, and his "own new purpose" is equally a work of art. Only when rewriting the work of another author in the same language[119] is it strictly appropriate to speak of a recomposition.[120]

8.3 The personal category of translation criticism

Let us summarize again the results of our consideration of the subjective limitations inherent in translation criticism. Translation criticism is always limited by the subjective conditions of the hermeneutical process and by the personality of the translator. Therefore especially in free renderings, although not exclusively, translation criticism should recognize the criteria of the personal category which should complement or replace the normal categories of translation criticism. It is precisely the personal category which restrains the critic from making absolute judgments. He can only oppose interpretation with interpretation, or artistic perspective with artistic perspective, comparing them and showing how they affect the original and the target language version. While such judgments are relative, as they must be, the criticism expressed remains objective (in the sense of not being arbitrary) because it is appropriate (in the sense of giving due consideration to personal implications). Ideally it may stimulate the reader of the criticism to form his own different and independent opinion.

---

[119] F. Kemp (1965, p. 17) mentions, for example, that Goethe would occasionally "take a friend's poetry and improve on it."

[120] Model approaches to the criticism of paraphrases and free renderings of literary works are discussed in connection with the personal category of translation criticism (although without naming criteria explicitly) in R.- R. Wuthenow (1969, chap. 3).

D. Conclusion

The foregoing discussions have addressed the potentials and limitations of a proper and objective translation criticism. The following thesis statements summarize the results of this discussion.

1. Translation criticism is proper if a *translation* (in the strict sense of the term) demanding a *text-oriented* translation method (accommodated to its text type) is examined by standards which are proper to its text type, i.e., when these criteria derive from the categories of the text type, the linguistic elements of the text, and the non-linguistic determinants that affect the text.

2. Translation criticism is proper if a *translation* (in the broader sense) demanding a *goal-oriented* translation method (directed to a special function or readership) is examined by criteria which are also derived from the functional category of translation criticism, adjusted to the standards of the special function or readership which the translation is intended to serve.

3. Both text-oriented and goal-oriented kinds of translation are affected by subjective influences: the subjective conditions of the hermeneutical process and of the translator's personality. Because the critic is also inevitably susceptible to the same influences, a personal category of translation criticism becomes an overruling component.

4. A proper translation criticism (whether text-oriented or goal-oriented) is accordingly objective only to the extent that it takes these subjective conditions into consideration.

References

Ayala, F. (1965). *Problemas de la traducción*. Madrid: Taurus Ediciones.

Bausch, K.R. (1963). *Verbum und verbale Periphrase im Französischen und ihre Transposition im Englischen, Deutschen und Spanischen*. Phil. Diss. Tübingen.

Benjamin, W. (1955). Die Aufgabe des Übersetzers. In Adorno, T. W. & Adorno, G. (Eds.), *Schriften*, vol. 1 (p. 40-54). Frankfurt: Suhrkamp (1923).

Blixen, O. (1954). *La traducción literaria y sus problemas*. Montevideo.

Bonse, M. (1968). *Carmen Laforet – Nada. Eine Übersetzungskritik*, Diploma thesis (Typescript). Heidelberg.

Borchardt, R. (1920). Nachwort zu einer Übertragung Die grossen Trobadors. In *Neue deutsche Beiträge*, vol. 2, no. 1.

Brang, P. (1963). Das Problem der Übersetzung in sowjetischer Sicht. In Störig, (1963) p. 410-427.

Brenner-Rademacher, S. (1965). Übersetzer sprachen mit Bühnenkünstlern. In *Babel, Revue Internationale de la Traduction*. Bonn: Internationale Vereinigung der Übersetzer (mit UNESCO).

Buber, M. (1963). Zu einer neuen Verdeutschung der Schrift. In Störig, (1963) p. 348-388.

Bühler, K. (1965). *Sprachtheorie*. Stuttgart. [(1990). *Theory of language: the representational function of language*. Philadelphia: Benjamins.]

Buschkiel, J. (1966, Mai 5). Wie man Theaterstücke überträgt. In *Die Welt*. Menschen und Ereignisse. Hamburg: Verlagshaus Die Welt.

Caillé, P. F. (1965). La traduction au cinéma. In Italiaander, (1965), p. 116-122.

Camba, J. (1947). *Alemania: impresiones de un Espanol*. Colección Austral 791. Buenos Aires: Espasa-Calpe Argentina.

Carnicé de Gállez, E. (1966). Observaciones sobre el aspecto sociolingüístico del lenguaje de la radio. In *Cuadernos del sur. Historia*, vol. 5 (p. 47-58). Bahía Blanca, Argentina: Departmento de Humanidades, Universidad Nacional de Sur.

Cary, E. (1963). *Die Zukunft*. In Störig, (1963) p. 389-394.

Catford, J.C. (1965). *A linguistic theory of translation: an essay in applied linguistics*. London: Oxford University.

Cela, C. J. (1945). *La familia de Pascual Duarte*. Buenos Aires. (1949). Übersetzung von George Leisewitz. *Durates Familie*. Hamburg.

[(1990). *The family of Pascual Duarte*. Boston: Little, Brown, and Co.]

Criado de Val, M. (1962). *Fisonomía del Idioma español; sus caracteristica comparades con las del frances, italiano, portugues, ingles y aleman*. Madrid: Aguilar.

Croce, B. (1953). *Poesia*. Bari: Laterza.

Delavenay, E. (1959). La machine á traduire. Paris. [(1960). *An introduction to machine translation*. New York: Praeger.]

Dietrich, G. (1955). *Erweiterte Form. Prateritum und Perfektum im Englischen: eine Aspekt-und Tempusstudie*. München: M. Hueber.

Dornseiff, F. (1959). *Der deutsche Wortschatz nach Sachgruppen*. Berlin: W. de Gruyter.

Erben, J. (1966). *Abriss der deutschen Grammatik*. 8th Edition. Berlin: Akadamie.

Feidel, G. (1970). *Technische Texte richtig übersetzen*. Düsseldorf, Wien: Econ-Verlag.

Foltin, H. F. (1968). Zur Erforschung der Unterhaltungs- und Trivialliteratur, insbesondere im Bereich des Romans. In H. O. Burger, (Ed.), *Studien zur Trvialliteratur* (p. 242-270). Frankfurt am Main: Klostermann.

Friedrich, H. (1965). Zur Frage der Übersetzungskunst. In *Sitzungsberichte der Heidelberger Akadamie der Wissenschaften, Philosophisch-historische Klasse*. Heidelberg: Winter.

Friedrich, W. (1969). *Technik des Übersetzens: Englisch and Deutsch. Eine systematische Anleitung für das Übersetzen ins Englische und ins Deutsche für Unterricht und Selbststudium*. München: Hueber.

Gadamer, H.-G. (1960). *Wahrheit und Methode. Gründzuge einer philosophischen Hermeneutik*. Tübingen. [(1998). *Truth and method*. (2nd rev. ed. Translation revised by Joel Weinsheimer and Donald G. Marshall). New York: Continuum.]

Goethe, J.W. (1962). *Dichtung und Wahrheit*. Deutsche Taschenbuch-Vereign. 3.11, vol. 24.

Goldenberg, B. (1963). *Lateinamerika und die kubanische Revolution*. Berlin: Köln.

Gorjan, Z. (1965). Über das akustische Element beim Übersetzen von Bühnenwerken. In R. Italiaander, p. 88-89.

Grimm, J. (1963). Über das pedantische in der deutschen Sprache. In Störig, (1963) p. 108-135.

Güttinger, F. (1963). *Zielsprache: Theorie und Technik des Übersetzens*. Zürich: Manesse.

von Haensch, G. (1968). Bemerkungen zur Übersetzungstechnik. Französisch/Deutsch. In *Idioma*, no. 2.

von Haensch, G. (1967). Wortbildung durch Ellipse im neuesten Französisch. In *Idioma*, no. 2.

Hartung, E. A. (1965). Was erwarten Theaterleute von einer Bühnenübersetzung. In *Babel, Revue Internationale de la Traduction*, vol. 2, no. 1 (p. 10-11).

Hayakawa, S. J. (n.d.). *Semantik*. Verlag Darmstadter Blatter, Deutsche Übersetzung. [(1952). *Semantics*. Indianapolis: Bobbs-Merrill.]

Hellwig, P. (1936). *Charakterologie*. (2nd rev. ed.). Stuttgart: E. Klett.

Hoeppener, C. (1953). Bemerkungen zur Übersetzung belletristischer Werke. In P. Topjer & C. Hoeppener, *Zur Frage der Übersetzung von schöner und wissenschaftlicher Literatur*. Berlin: Verlag Kultur und Fortschritt.

Hortelano, J. G. (1962). *Tormento de verano*. Barcelona. German translation: Sommergewitter.

von Humboldt, W. (1963). Einleitung zu Agamemnon. In Störig, (1963) p. 71-96.

Italiaander, R. (Ed.). (1965). *Übersetzen. Vorträge und Beiträge vom Internationalen Kongress literarischer Übersetzer in Hamburg 1965*. Frankfurt am Main: Athenäum.

Jumpelt, R. W. (1961). *Die Übersetzung naturwissenschaftlicher und technischer Literatur: sprachliche Massstäbe und Methoden zur Bestimmung ihrer Wesenszüge und Probleme*. Langenscheidt Bibliothek für Wissenschaft und Praxis, vol. 1. Berlin-Schöneberg: Langenscheidt.

Kade. O. (1964). *Subjecktive und objective Faktoren im Übersetzungsprozess*. Phil. Diss. (Typescript), Leipzig.

Kann, H. J. (1968). *Übersetzungsprobleme in den deutschen Übersetzungen von drei anglo-amerikanischen Kurzgeschichten: Aldous Huxleys "Green tunnels," Ernest Hemingways "The Killers" und "A Clean, Well-Lighted Place."* Mainzer amerikanistische Beiträge, vol. 10. München: M. Hueber.

Kellner, H. (1964). Übersetzung und Sinnklarung. Ein Beitrag zur Übersetzungskritik. In *Lebende Sprachen*, vol. 3 (p. 87-90). Berlin: Langensheidt.

Kemp, F. (1947). Vom Übersetzen. In *Deutsche Beiträge zur geistigen Überlieferung*, vol. 1, no. 2, (p. 147-158). Heidelberg: Lothar Stiehm.

Kemp, F. (1965). *Kunst und Vergnügen des Übersetzens*. Opuscula aus Wissenschaft und Dichtung, 24. Pfullingen: Neske.

Kloepfer, R. (1967). *Die Theorie der literarischen Übersetzung. Romanisch-deutscher Sprachbereich.* Freiburger Schriften zur romanischen Philologie, vol. 12. München: Fink.

Korlén, G. (1966). Konstruktive Übersetzungskritik als Aufgabe der Schwedischen Universitätsgermanistik. In *Babel, Revue Internationale de la Traduction*, vol. 12, no. 1 (p. 26-31).

Koschmieder, E. (1955). Das Problem der Übersetzung. In H. Krahe, *Corolla linguistica. Festschrift Ferdinand Sommer zum 80. Geburtstag. Mai 1955, Dargebracht von Freunden, Schülern und Kollegen.* Wiesbaden: O. Harrassowitz.

Laforet, C. (1963). *Nada.* Barcelona. (1959). Übersetzung von Raimund Lackenbucher. Köln. [(1958). *Nada.* London: Weidenfeld and Nicolson.]

Lausberg, H. (1960). *Handbuch der literarischen Rhetorik.* München. [(1998). *Handbook of literary rhetoric: A foundation for literary study.* Leiden: Brill.]

de Lera, A. M. (1968, Feb. 29). La oratoria. In *ABC*, Mirador Literario, Suplemento Semanal de Crítica e Información.

Lessing, G.E. (1767-1768). Die Kunst der Übersetzung. Bavarian Academy of Fine Arts. [(1879). *The Hamburg Dramaturgy*, no. 8. München: Bayerische Akademie der Schönen Kunst.].

Lessing, G. E. (n.d.). *Schriften zur Literatur. Ausgewählte Werke*, vol. 6 (Goldmanns Gelbe Taschenbücher vol. 1851). München.

Levý, J. (1968). Die Übersetzung von Theaterstucken. In *Babel, Revue Internationale de la Traduction*, vol. 14 (p. 77-82).

Luther, A. (1949). Die Kunst des Übersetzens. In A. Luther, (Ed.), *Studien zur deutschen Dichtung*, Essais (p. 9-27). Kuppenheim Murgtal: E. F. Krehbiel.

Luther, M. (1963). Sendbrief vom Dolmetschen. In Störig, (1963) p. 14-32.

MacDermott, D. (1969). What man has made of beast. In *Idioma*, no. 2.

Mager, L. (1968). *La familia de Pascual Duarte – Duartes Familie.* Eine Übersetzungskritik, Diploma Thesis (Typescript). Heidelberg.

Malblanc, A. (1961). *Stylistique comparée du français et de l'allemand; essai de representation linguistique comparée et étude de traduction.* Paris: Didier.

Merian-Genast, E. (1958). Französische und deutsche Übersetzungskunst. In *Forschungsprobleme der vergleichenden Literaturgeschichte.* 2nd series (p. 25-38). Tübingen.

Mounin, G. (1967). *Die Übersetzung. Geschichte, Theorie, Anwendung.* München: Nymphenburger.

Murray, D. C. (1968). The adventures of Mr. Bodidioms. In *Idioma*, no. 2 (p.52-59).

Nida, E. A. (1964). *Toward a science of translating, with special reference to principles and procedures involved in Bible translating*. Leiden: E. J. Brill.

Nida, E. A. & Taber, C. R. (1969). *Theorie und Praxis des Übersetzens: unter besonderer Berücksichtigung der Bibelübersetzung*. Stuttgart: Weltbund der Bibelgesellschaften. [(1974). *The Theory and Practice of Translation*. Leiden: E. J. Brill.]

Nossack, H. E. (1965). Übersetzen und übersetzt werden. In Italiaander, (1965) p. 9-18.

Oettinger, A. G. (1963). Das Problem der Übersetzung. In Störig, (1963) p. 436-467.

Ortega y Gasset, J. (1937). *Miseria y esplendor de la traducción. Elend und Glanz der Übersetzung*. La Nacion (Buenos Aries) May-June. München: Langewiesche. [Reprinted *Obras Completas*, vol. 5 p. 427-448. Madrid: Revista de Occidente, 1946-47.]

Pelster, T. (1966). *Die politische Rede im Westen und Osten Deutschlands. Vergleichende Stiluntersuchung mit beigefügten Texten*. Supplement to *Zeitschrift Wirkendes Wort* 14. Düsseldorf: Padagogischer Verlag Schwann.

Pörtner, R. (1968). Ich schreibe ein Sachbuch. In *Westermanns Monatshefte*, vol.109, no. 4.

Politzer, R. L. (1966). Zur sprachwissenschaftlichen Einteilung der Übersetzungsprobleme. In *Lebende Sprachen*, vol. 11, no. 2. Berlin: Langenscheidt.

Porzig, W. (1962). *Das Wunder der Sprache: Probleme, Methoden und Ergebnisse der modernen Sprachwissenschaft*. Bern; München: Francke.

von Radecki, S. (1965). Vom Übersetzen. In *Die Kunst der Übersetzung*, 8. Folge des *Jahrbuchs Gestalt und Gedanke*. München: R. Oldenbourg.

Reich-Ranicki, M. (1965). Verräter, Brückenbauer, Waisenkinder. In Italiaander, (1965) p. 69-73.

Reiss, K. (1967, August). Übersetzungsprobleme: Die Übertragung von Wortspielen. In *Der Übersetzer. Diskussionsbeiträge und Informationen*, vol. 4, no. 8.

Reiss, K. (1968). Überlegungen zu einer Theorie der Übersetzungskritik. In *Linguistica Antverpiensia*, vol. 2 (p. 369-383). Antwerp: Rijksuniversitair Centrum Antwerpen, Hoger Instituut voor Vertalers en Tolken.

Reiss, K. (1969). Textbestimmung und Übersetzungsmethode. Entwurf einer Texttypologie. In *Ruperto Carola*, yr. 21, vol. 46 (p. 69-75). Heidelberg: Vereinigung der Freunde der Studentenschaft der Universität Heidelberg.

Rohner, L. (1966). *Der deutsche Essay*. Berlin: Luchterhand.

Rosenzweig, F. (1926). *Die Schrift und Luther*. Berlin: Schocken.

Sánchez, Ferlosio R. (1956). *El Jarama*. Barcelona. [(1962). *The one day of the week*. New York: Abelard-Schuman.]

Savory, T. H. (1958). *The Art of Translation*. Philadelphia: DuFour.

Schadewaldt, W. (1963). Das Problem des Übersetzens. In Störig, (1963) p. 249-267.

Schadewaldt, W. (1964). *Griechisches Theater*. Frankfurt am Main.

von Schlegel, A. W. (1846). *Gesammelte Werke*. Ed. E. Böcking. Leipzig.

von Schlegel, A. W. (1963). Über die Bhagavad-Gita. In Störig, (1963) p. 97-100.

Schleiermacher, F. (1963). Über die verschiedenen Methoden des Übersetzens. In Störig, (1963) p. 38-70.

Schneider, H. (1956). Null-acht fünfzehn und Cero-ocho quince, ein kritischer Beitrag zum Problem der literarischen Übersetzung. In *Romanistisches Jahrbuch*, vol. 7, 1955-1956 (p. 332-357). Hamburg.

Schottlaender, R. (1966). *Einleitung zur Sophokles-Ausgabe*. (p. XXV-XXXVII). Berlin.

Seco, R. (1954). *Manual de gramática española*. Madrid: Aguilar.

Seibel, E. A. (1963). *Einige Aspekte der Komik in spanischen modismos*. Phil. Diss., Köln.

Spranger, E. (1920). *Lebensformen. Geisteswissenschaftliche Psychologie und Ethik der Persönlichkeit*. Halle: M. Niemeyer.

Störig, H.- J. (Ed.). (1963). *Das Problem des Übersetzens*. Stuttgart: H. Goverts.

Süskind, W. E. (1959). Die Erfahrungen eines literarischen Übersetzers. In *Lebende Sprachen*, no. 3. Berlin: Langenscheidt.

Süskind, W. E. & von der Vring, G. (1963). *Die Kunst der Übersetzung*. München: R. Oldenbourg.

Tabernig de Pucciarelli, E. (1964). Aspectos técnicos y literarios de la traducción. In *Boletín de estudios germánicos*, vol. 5 (p. 137, 155). Mendoza, Argentina: Universidad Nacional de Cuyo, Facultad de Filosofia y Letras, Instituto de Literaturas Modernas, Seccion de Literatura Alemana.

Thieme, K. (1956). Das Problem der sachverständigen öffentlichen Kritik an Buchübersetzungen. In *Lebende Sprachen*, vol. 1 (p. 27 f.).

Berlin: Langenscheidt.

von Tscharner, E. H. (1963). Chinesische Gedichte in deutscher Sprache. In Störig, (1963) p.268-298. [First published 1932 in *Ostasiatische Zeitschrift*, 18 NF 8, p. 189-209.]

Wandruszka, M. (1969). *Sprachen, vergleichbar und unvergleichlich.* München: R. Piper.

Weinrich, H. (1966). *Linguistik der Lüge.* Heidelberg: L. Schneider.

Weisgerber, L. (1961). Vertragstexte als sprachliche Aufgabe (Formulierungs-, Auslegungs-, und Übersetzungsprobleme des Südtirol-Abkommens von 1946). In *Sprachforum*, Zeitschrift fur angewandte Sprachwissenschaft, Suppl. 1. Bonn: H. Bouvier u. Co. Verlag, etc.

Widmer, W. (1959). *Fug und Unfug des Übersetzens. Sachlich-polemische Betrachtungen zu einem literarischen Nebengeleise.* Köln; Berlin: Kiepenheuer & Witsch.

von Wilamowitz-Moellendorff, U. (1963). Was ist Übersetzens? In Störig, (1963) p. 139-169.

Wirl, J. (1958). *Grundsätzliches zur Problematik des Dolmetschens und des Übersetzens.* Wien; Stuttgart: W. Braumuller.

Wuthenow, R-R. (1969). *Das fremde Kunstwerk; Aspekte der literarischen Übersetzung.* Palaestra, vol. 252. Göttingen: Vandenhoeck & Ruprecht.

Index